SAMUEL

Israel's rejection of God and his prophet Samuel, the betrayal of Saul, the reluctant king, and the secret anointing of the charismatic David. Samuel describes how the ruthless warrior wins the two kingdoms of Judah and Israel, suffers a series of heartbreaking tragedies as the consequence of his seduction of Bathsheba and the murder of her innocent husband, Uriah, one of the king's mighty officers. Ambition, lust, assassinations, rebellions and political intrigue are the ingredients which make the *Book of Samuel* in this faithful but interpretative translation as gripping a tale as Robert Graves's *I Claudius*.

SIDNEY BRICHTO *is a leading liberal Jewish Rabbi and theologian who writes and lectures on Jewish, religious and moral issues.*

Published jointly with the *Books of Samuel*
in the first series of The People's Bible are:
Genesis
The Books of Samuel
Songs of Songs

The People's Bible

Samuel

BOOKS I & II

newly translated by Sidney Brichto

Sinclair-Stevenson

First published in Great Britain by
Sinclair-Stevenson
3 South Terrace, London SW7 2TB

British Library Cataloguing in Publication Data
A CIP catalogue record for this book is available from
The British Library.

ISBN 0 953 739 81 3

Typeset by Rowland Phototypesetting Ltd. Bury St Edmunds, Suffolk.
Printed and bound by Mackays of Chatham plc, Kent.

This new interpretative translation is dedicated to the memory of my brother, Chanan Herbert Brichto. He loved the Bible with enormous passion not for its historical veracity but for its moral and literary genius. His seminal books 'Towards a Grammar of Political Poetics' and 'The Names of God' will, I am convinced, in time revolutionize biblical scholarship. His respect, bordering on worship, of those geniuses who were the vehicles of the Still Small Voice of God, is what inspired me to make this attempt to give the Bible back to the people of great, little, or no faith.

I want to thank Christopher Sinclair-Stevenson whose faith in the project never wavered when my own began to ebb. This attempt is as much his creation as mine. I thank Beverley Taylor, my personal assistant for so many years, for her dedication and help in enabling me to fulfil my creative interests; and to my wife and children for their advice and patience in my pursuit of this ambitious project. Finally, to John Porter goes my own and Christopher's gratitude, for without his vision Genesis and the accompanying volumes might never have seen the light of day.

SIDNEY BRICHTO

Preface

The simple purpose of this new Bible is to give it back to people who welcome a good story, fine poetry, and inspiration. For too long now, the Bible has become the best-seller least read. There are several reasons for this, foremost among them the claim of believers that the Bible was written or inspired by God. As our age has become increasingly secular such a claim has turned people away. Also, atheists and humanists maintain that the Bible is a pack of distortions and false prophecies which prevent men and women from accepting their full responsibility for human destiny.

Literate people, however, aware of the Bible as a great classic, feel obligated to read it. Most do not get very far. Repetitions, lack of chronological order, tedious genealogical inserts, stories which cry out for explanations which are not given, incomprehensible thoughts – all these elements, as well as the formal divisions into chapters and verses, have forced most readers to give up even before they have reached the middle of the first book of Genesis.

The purpose of this edition of the Bible is to recast it in such a manner as to make it readable. It will be the complete biblical text faithfully translated after reference to other translations. The biblical narrative style is so sparse that it leaves much to the imagination. This provides a challenge to consider what the author has left out. On occasion, the editor will respond by interacting with the text to fill out the story. To avoid confusion, such elaborations will be indicated by a different print font. This is done with the expectation that some readers will feel that they (and indeed they may be right) could have done better. Such reactions are welcome and proof that the editor's objective of making the Bible come alive has been achieved. Material which appears irrelevant and interrupts the flow is moved into an appendix. Words and sentences will be added, also in a different print font, when necessary to provide continuity and to remove seeming contradictions. references will abound, to enable the reader to find the place in a traditional Bible should he or she wish to make comparisons.

Since the Bible is a library of books, each book or group of books will therefore require special treatment, with a specific introduction to explain how the editor has dealt with the material in his attempt to enable you not only to possess a Bible but to read it with comprehension and even with pleasure.

The Name of God

The name of God as it appears in the Bible is YHVH (Hebrew script has no vowels). This is the ineffable name which was always read as Adonai, meaning 'my Lord'. The traditional translation of YHVH is therefore Lord. The Jerusalem Bible translation refers to God as Yahweh which most scholars believe was the pronunciation of the four consonants. I was tempted to follow this example, because the name makes God into a vital personality – the major protagonist in Israel's history – rather than an abstract force. Cautious respect for tradition made me hold to 'the Lord', but I hope that the reader will remember that the Lord, the God of Israel, is portrayed as a personality revealing the full range of emotions: paternal justice, maternal compassion, love and reason, regret and anger, punishing and forgiving.

Introduction

"No other Old Testament story apart from the legend of Adam and Eve," writes Jonathan Keates about the books of Samuel, "has tugged so hard at the narrative imagination. The hold of these two books on the reader, whatever their basis in fact, is a novelist's or a playwright's rather than that of an historian. This is the earliest surviving prose narrative whose author has grasped the importance of motivation and emotional consistency in bringing characters credibly to life."

It is the truth of this observation which has made me wonder why these books have never been considered as great literary classics, but only as part of the history of Israel. This is the saddest example of how inclusion in the Bible can prevent great writing from achieving proper study as creative literature. I have read the books many times, and each time am thrilled by the purity and directness of their descriptions and dialogue.

The fact that this historical romance found its way into the holy canon can be attributed to two factors. The first is that God is given the role of leading hero. It is he who moves the plot along determining the success and failure of the human protagonists with inexplicable changes of attitude, more consistent with the vagaries of the human heart than that of a perfect deity. Of course, this is what makes him into a personality who requires as much analysis as do Samuel, Saul, David and Joab and other leading characters. All are full of human contradictions, wavering between the polarities of love and hate, duty and the pleasure principle, compassion and brutality, humility and overriding arrogance and ambition.

The second factor which enabled it to be canonized, helped perhaps by 'religious' inserts in the course of its many editions, was the validation of the Jewish prophetic doctrine – that God alone is the ruler of the world and that the appointment of a human monarch of the tribes of Israel was a compromise demanded by an undisciplined people with insufficient faith in the source of their deliverance from Egypt and their conquest of the Promised Land. It is this contest between God and Man, the prophet and king, which creates such ambivalent attitudes to Saul, an innocent country lad who did not wish to be king but had kingship thrust upon him. Once he begins to enjoy its pomp, glory and power, the prophet Samuel who insisted he become king behaves erratically towards him – first betraying him and then mourning over his rejection by God.

The conflicting sides of Samuel's character are mirrored in Saul, in David and even in Joab, his mighty commander-in-chief. David knows that he has been anointed to be Saul's successor but swears his utter loyalty to his sovereign and twice refuses to harm him. Is he prepared to wait for his karma to be realized? Saul, rejected by Samuel and feeling in his bones that David is his chosen successor, seeks his death, but without proof for his suspicions. Adding to his heavy emotional burden is the tragic irony that Jonathan, the son to whom he wishes to pass on his kingdom, is enchanted by David, and swears an oath of loyalty to him. How the narrator expresses the many faces of his heroes is what makes them as interesting and problematic as Hamlet and King Lear. The reader must not be sidetracked from the appreciation of these compelling figures by the miraculous events which fill the narrative. After all, God, as the major hero, also has to enter into play, and how can he do so except through the performance of signs and wonders, appropriate to his divine power?

It is a pity that Robert Graves never put his hand to the books of Samuel as he did to Plutarch and Suetonius to create his masterpieces, *I Claudius* and *Claudius the God*. Had he done so, more people would have turned to the original if only to see how authentic his version was.

For the moment, readers must be satisfied with this new translation whose major purpose is to make them pick up the story and wish to read it to its conclusion. To do this, without omission and maintaining a loyalty to the text, I have moved certain episodes to the appendix. I have also added, as the general preface says, in a different print font certain interventions to give flesh to the episodes. I do this not to compete with the original narrator, but to show how much can be added by the interested and creative reader. Do not for a moment think that I am suggesting that my own interaction with the text is the only one or the best. For example, why Uriah did not return to Bathsheba's bosom when King David urged him to do so is a mystery to us today as it must have been to David. It is these enigmas of human nature, of the motives for human behaviour, which remain the challenge of all great works of literature.

Index of Major Episodes

The birth of Samuel

Now there was a man from Ramataim, a Zuphite from the hill
country of Ephraim named Elkanah ben[1] Jeroham ben Elihu ben
Tohu, ben Zuph, an Ephramite. He had two wives. The name of
one was Hannah, the other Peninah. She had children but
Hannah had none.

That same man would go up from his city year by year to worship
and offer sacrifices to the LORD of Hosts[2] in Shiloh. The two sons
of Eli, Hophni and Phinehas were priests to the LORD on the days
when Elkanah made a sacrificial feast; he gave shares to his wife
Peninah and to all her sons and daughters. To Hannah he also
gave a single share, but twice the size because Hannah was the
one he loved. **He was sad for her because she had no children to
receive their portions** for the LORD had closed her womb. Her rival
for the affections of her husband taunted her to humiliate her
because the LORD had made her barren. This went on year after
year when she went to the house of the LORD, she always taunted
her, so she wept and did not eat. **Seeing this and understanding
her heartache because she was barren,** he consoled her, "Why
do you cry and why do you not eat? Why do you let your heart
grieve? Am I not better to you than ten sons?" After they had
eaten and drank at Shiloh, Hannah left them. Eli the priest was
sitting on his chair by the doorpost of the temple of the LORD. In
her distress she prayed to the LORD as she wept bitterly. She cried

[1] Ben means 'son of'. The English equivalent of ben Jehoram would be
Jehoramson like Stevenson. I have not translated 'ben' whenever it occurs as
'son of' but have kept to the Hebrew *ben.*
[2] Yahweh Zebaioth, meaning the Lord of the armies of Israel and the armies of
heaven: the sun, moon and stars.

out her vow: "LORD OF HOSTS, if you will look upon the suffering of your servant and take notice of me and regard your servant to give her a male child, I will give him to the LORD for the whole of his life and a razor will not touch his head."[1]

She prayed a long time before the LORD. Eli was studying her face. Hannah was thinking to herself, her lips were quivering without her voice being heard. Eli thought that she was drunk and reprimanded her, "How long will you be drunk? Do not let your wine take control over you." But Hannah spoke up, "That is not so, my lord. I am a heartbroken woman. I have drunk no wine or spirits. I was pouring out my soul before the LORD. Do not think me a shameless woman. It is out of my distress and utter frustration that I have been speaking to myself in this way."

Eli then answered her, "Go in peace. May the God of Israel grant your petition." She replied, "May your servant be worthy of your kindness." So the woman went on her way and she ate and drank and no longer wore an unhappy face. They rose up early in the morning, worshipped the LORD, set off on their return and arrived home in Ramah.

Elkanan made love to Hannah his wife. The LORD remembered her **prayer**. Hannah conceived and at the turn of the year bore a son. She named him Samuel because, "I asked the LORD for him."[2]

---

[1] She will make him into a Nazirite, a person dedicated to God's service whose hair could not be cut. The laws of the Nazirite are found in Numbers 6:5. Samson was a Nazirite. Once his hair was cut by Delilah, he lost his divine power.

[2] The name Samuel means "God heard". A more appropriate name would have been Saul which is derived from the verb: ask. While visiting a bible class of my brother's at Hebrew Union College, I heard him teaching this episode and he remarked that this was a cryptic allusion to the fact that Samuel's main role would be the appointment of Saul as the first king of Israel.

Hannah then told Elkanah of her vow to give her son to the Lord. He asked her:
- "Why have you done so? It was a rash vow."
- "Because I wanted a son, to feel a child in my belly. I prayed and prayed but the Lord did not hear my prayer. When I vowed to give my son to him, only then did I conceive."
- "But what good is this child to you if he is to be taken away from you? It was a rash vow. Because you have not told me and he is my son the law is that I can annul your vow before the Lord and you will be guiltless. Let me do this so that our son may be with us."
- "No, but I shall give my son to the Lord. If I withhold him and keep him close to my breast, the Lord may strike him down and I will be bereft."

The man Elkanah with his entire household went up to make a sacrifice to the LORD and to fulfil his vows. Hannah, however, did not go up because she said to her husband, "When the child is weaned, only then will I bring him, that he may be presented to the LORD – then, there will he stay forever." Elkanah agreed with her, "Do what you think best. Remain until you have weaned him. Then will the LORD enable you to fulfil your vows." The woman waited and nursed her son and waited until she weaned him.

When she weaned him she took him with her along with a three-year-old bullock, one bushel of flour and a bottle of wine. She brought him to the house of the LORD in Shiloh; the child was very young. After the bullock had been slaughtered she brought the child to Eli, saying to him, "Please, my lord, by the life of my lord, I am the woman who stood by you at this very place to pray to the LORD. It was for this boy that I prayed. The LORD granted me what I asked of him. Therefore I now tend[1] him

---

[1] The root of "to tend" (sha-al) in Hebrew is the same as that of 'to ask'.
Hannah is poetically offering God a *quid pro quo:* "I asked, you gave, and I give him back to you as a permanent loan.

to the LORD. As long as he lives, he is on loan to the LORD." They bowed down there before the LORD. Hannah prayed **to the Lord with a psalm**[1] . Elkanah **and Hannah** went home to Ramah, but the boy went into the service of the LORD under **the supervision** of Eli, the priest.

The sons of Eli, **Hophni and Phinehas** however, were complete rogues, with no respect for the LORD nor for their priestly obligations to the people. **For example,** whenever a man offered a sacrifice, a servant of the priest came, while the flesh was still boiling, and he plunged a three-pronged fork into the pot, pan, cauldron or basin. All that the fork brought up the priest would keep. This was done at Shiloh to all the Israelites who came there. But, the servant of Hophni and Phinehas, even before the fat was burnt would come and say to the man who was sacrificing, "Give me flesh to roast for the priest for he won't accept boiled meat, only raw meat." **Now this was a desecration because the sacrifice had to remain whole until it was cooked and the parts consecrated to God were burnt.** If the man protested to him, "Let the meat boil first, then take as much as you want," the reply would be: "No, give it now, if not – I will take it by force." So the sins of the young men were grievous before the LORD for they treated the offerings to the LORD with contempt.

Samuel, however, was a young attendant in the LORD's service. **He stayed away from Hophni and Phinehas, the sons of Eli, for their evil ways frightened him. He longed for his mother and father. He could not understand why he had been forsaken.** He was dressed in a linen apron. His mother would make for him a little robe which she brought to him year by year when she went up with her husband to offer up their annual sacrifice, **to see Samuel and to bring him presents**. Eli would bless Elkanah and his wife, "The LORD give you children from this woman, in place

---

[1] See Appendix 1 for Psalm: I Samuel 2:1–10

of the loan of Samuel which she made to the LORD." Then they would return to their own place. The LORD remembered Hannah; she conceived, bearing three sons and two daughters. **She and her husband praised the Lord.**

The boy Samuel was growing up in the service of the LORD. Now Eli, being very old, heard what his sons were doing to all the Israelites and how they were lying with the women who gathered for worship at the very entrance of the Tent of Meeting.[1] He berated them, "Why do you do such things? I hear of your wicked deeds from everyone. No, my sons, the report I hear being spread by the LORD's people is not a good one. **Consider,** if one man sins against another, God will judge, but if a man sins against the LORD who will pray for him?" They did not listen to their father's voice. **In any event it was too late.** The LORD had decided to slay them. Samuel, however, was growing up in stature and in esteem both with the LORD and the people of Israel.

Now, a man of God came to Eli. He said to him, "Thus said the LORD, 'I revealed myself to your father's family when they were in Egypt subject to the House of Pharaoh. I chose him out of all the tribes of Israel to be my priest, to go up to my altar, to burn incense, to wear a priestly apron in my presence. I granted to your father's house the privilege of offering sacrifices on behalf of the Israelites. Why therefore do you trample upon my sacrifices and my offerings that I have commanded in my dwelling? You respect your sons more than me, so that you can fatten yourselves from the best of the offerings of Israel, my people.' Therefore, this is the oracle of the LORD, the God of Israel: 'I had promised that your descendants and your father's descendants would minister before me forever.' This is the oracle of the LORD, 'This is what I ordain. Those who honour me will I honour and those who

---

[1] *Ohel Moed* – The tent appointed for worship at Festivals etc. which contained the Holy Ark.

despise me will be despised. Lo, the days are coming that I will cut off your strength and the strength of your father's house. No man will reach old age in your family. You will suffer with envy to see Israel's prosperity while no man of your family will live to an old age. Still, I will not cut off every one of your descendants from my altar but your eyes will grow dim, and your heart weary. Your offspring will die as commoners. This is the omen for you: Your two sons, Hophni and Phinehas, will die on the same day. But I will raise up for myself a faithful priest who will act in accordance with my heart and soul. I will faithfully establish his descendants perpetually to minister before my anointed king.[1] **But as for the fate** of your descendants those who survive will go down on their knees before him for a pittance of silver and a piece of bread and plead: 'Give me, I beg of you some priestly duty that I may earn myself some scraps of food.' "

Samuel becomes the Lord's Prophet

The boy Samuel was ministering to the LORD before Eli. In those days the word of the LORD was rarely heard and visions were not common. On that particular day, while Eli was lying down in his usual place – his eyes had become so dim that he could hardly see. The lamp of God was still burning and Samuel was sleeping in the temple of the LORD where the Ark of God was. The LORD called Samuel and he said, "Here I am," and he ran to Eli and said: "Here I am, for you called me." He replied, "I called you not, go back to sleep." He went and lay down again. The LORD called Samuel yet again. Samuel got up, went to Eli saying, "Here I am because you called me." He said, "No, I did not call you,

---

[1] As this is an historical novel, one can look ahead and surmise that the writer is signalling that there will emerge a priestly family who will serve God alongside his appointed kings. But, the fact that God will interpret the people's desire for a king as a rejection of his own monarchy would indicate that this oracle is a later insertion.

my son, go and sleep." This was before Samuel had experienced the LORD, before the oracle of the LORD had been revealed to him. When the LORD called Samuel a third time, he got up and went to Eli: "Here I am because you did call me." Eli then understood that the LORD was calling the boy. Eli instructed Samuel, "Go, lie down, when you are called, you must say, 'Speak, O LORD, for your servant is listening.'" Samuel returned to his place and lay down.

The LORD came and this time stood there and called as before, "Samuel, Samuel." "Speak, for your servant is listening," Samuel replied. The LORD said to Samuel, "Behold, I will do a thing in Israel that will make both ears of all who hear of it ring. On that day I will fulfil against Eli all that I have said about his family from the beginning of my words to the end of them, for I have told him that I will condemn his family forever for the iniquities of which he was aware – how his sons blasphemed against me and he did not sufficiently rebuke them. Therefore, I have sworn against Eli's House – no sacrifices or offerings will ever expiate the guilt of Eli's house."

Now, Samuel lay there until morning when he opened the doors of the LORD's house. And Samuel **did not go to attend to his master because he** was frightened to recount the vision to him. Eli summoned Samuel saying, "Samuel, my son." He replied, "I am here." He asked, "What did he say to you? Please hold back nothing from me. God do to you **what I fear he intends to do against me** and even worse, if you hide from me anything he said to you." Samuel told him everything and withheld nothing from him. **After Samuel had told him everything,** he said, "He is the LORD, he will act according to his pleasure."

So Samuel grew up and the LORD was with him. He did not allow any of Samuel's prophecies to be unfulfilled. Thus all Israel from Dan to Beersheba knew that Samuel was destined to be the LORD's prophet. The LORD continued to have a presence in Shiloh because the LORD revealed through Samuel in Shiloh the oracles of the LORD. The fame of Samuel's oracles spread throughout the land of Israel.

The Glory of Israel has gone into exile

At the time that the Philistines gathered for war against Israel, she went out to engage the Philistines in battle. They made camp at Eben-ezer; the Philistines encamped at Aphek. The Philistines began the attack against the Israelites. The battle was fierce. Israel was routed by the Philistines; some four thousand men were killed on the battlefield. The Israelite troops returned to their camp. The elders of Israel asked, "Why has the LORD allowed us to be defeated by the Philistines? Let us send for the Ark of the Covenant of the LORD from Shiloh; thus, he will be among us and save us from the hands of our enemies."

The troops sent men to Shiloh. Hophni and Phinehas, Eli's two sons, were custodians of the Ark of the Covenant of the LORD. They brought down the Ark of the Covenant of the LORD: He who is enthroned between the Cherubim.[1] When the Ark of the Covenant of the LORD entered the camp, all the Israelites gave a great shout so that the ground shook. The Philistines heard the sound of the shouting. They asked, "Why is there such great shouting in the camp of the Hebrews?" When they heard that the Ark of the LORD had come into the camp, the Philistines were terrified for they thought, "God has come to the camp." They cried, "We are in trouble; this has never happened before. We are in trouble; who will save us from the power of this mighty

---

[1] The Cherubim were not child angels. Most likely they were winged animals with human faces revealing the essence of the ruler's power. The wings of the Cherubim may have touched each other making a space for the invisible God to sit.

God? He is the same God who struck down the Egyptians with every kind of affliction in the wilderness."

But the Lords of the five cities of the Philistines encouraged them, "Take heart and act like men, O Philistines, or you will become slaves to the Hebrews as they have been slaves to you. Be men and fight!" The Philistines joined battle but the LORD did not save Israel because of the sins of Hophni and Phinehas, Eli's sons. Israel was defeated. They all fled to their homes. The defeat was very great. Thirty thousand foot soldiers of Israel fell; the Ark of God was also captured and Eli's two sons, Hophni and Phinehas were slain.

A Benjaminite fled from the battlefield, reaching Shiloh the same day. As signs of mourning, his clothes were rent and dirt was on his head. When he arrived, Eli was sitting on his chair, waiting by the road. His heart trembled because of the Ark of the LORD. **He feared that the glory of Israel was taken from Israel.** When the man came into the city to bring the news, the whole town broke out in a great wail. Eli heard the sound of the outcry and asked, "What does this great uproar mean?" The man ran quickly over to tell Eli – now Eli was ninety-eight years old and his eyes were set in a blank stare – and said to him, "I am he who has come from the war, I have just fled from the battlefield." He asked, "What has happened, my son?" The news-bearer replied, "Israel fled from before the Philistines, the troops have also been slaughtered, your two sons, Hophni and Phinehas, are dead and the Ark of God has been taken captive." When the Ark of God was mentioned, Eli fell backward off his seat by the gate, broke his neck and died for he was an old man and large. He had been Israel's chieftain for forty years.

His daughter-in-law, the wife of Phinehas, was about to give birth. When she heard the news that the Ark of God had been taken, that both her father-in-law and husband were dead, her labour pains came upon her, she crouched down and gave birth. As she was dying from the premature birth, those standing by her comforted her. "Do not be afraid for you have given birth to a son."[1] But she did not answer nor did she accept any comfort. Before she died, she named the boy Ichabod[2], thinking, the glory of Israel has gone into exile because the Ark of God had been taken and because of the deaths of her father-in-law and husband. She said, "The Glory of Israel has gone into exile because the Ark of God has been taken into captivity."

The Ark of God is returned

The Philistines took the Ark of God from Eben-ezer to Ashdod to the Temple of Dagon[3] and placed it near the statue of Dagon. The next day when the citizens of Ashdod awoke **they found that** Dagon had fallen face to the ground before the Ark of the LORD. They raised Dagon and returned him to his place. The next morning they found that Dagon had fallen face down before the Ark of the LORD but the head of Dagon and its two hands lay severed on the threshold. Only **the fish trunk of** Dagon was intact. It is for this reason that the priests of Dagon and all who enter Dagon's Temple in Ashdod will not tread on the threshold to this very day.

The hand of the LORD was very severe upon the citizens of Ashdod. He devastated them **with swarms of rats** and afflicted them with haemorrhoids throughout the city and its suburbs.[4] When the

[1] The comfort is that she will achieve immortality through her son. The belief that one lived through one's children was as strong then as it is today.
[2] English meaning is "No glory".
[3] Their major god – half man, half fish.
[4] My intervention **with swarms of rats** while not in the Hebrew text is justified by the Septuagint, the translation of the Bible in ancient Greek and what follows later in the story. Instead of haemorrhoids, many translate the Hebrew to read tumours. Both could be the result of a bubonic plague caused by the

men of Ashkelon saw what was happening, they exclaimed, "The Ark of the God of Israel should not stay with us for his hand is hard upon us and upon Dagon our god." They summoned and assembled all the lords of the Philistines to decide, "What shall we do with the Ark of the God of Israel?" They decided, "Let the Ark of the God of Israel be taken to Gath." So they moved the Ark of the God of Israel to Gath.

After they had moved it to Gath, the hand of the LORD struck the city causing a very great panic. He struck the citizens young and old and they were afflicted by haemorrhoids. So they sent off the Ark of God to Ekron. When it arrived, the citizens of Ekron cried out, shouting, "They have brought us the Ark of the God of Israel to slay us and our people." Once again they summoned and assembled all the lords of the Philistines, demanding, "Send away the Ark of the God of Israel. Let it return to its home so that neither we nor our people die." For there was a panic of death throughout the city. Indeed, the hand of God was very severe there. The people who escaped death were smitten by haemorrhoids. The cry of the city was so great that it reached the heavens.

The Ark of the LORD was in Philistine territory for seven months. Finally, the Philistines took counsel with the priests and diviners, "What shall we do with the Ark of the LORD? Tell us how shall we return it to where it belongs?" They answered, "If you intend to send back the Ark of the God of Israel, do not send it back empty-handed. Return it with a generous guilt offering. Then, if you are healed, you will know that he did not remove his powerful hand from afflicting you because you took his ark." They asked, "What guilt offering shall we pay him?" They replied, "According to the number of the lords of the Philistines, five golden images

rats. I have kept 'haemorrhoids' as I believe that the author was seeking to make fun of the Philistines. Such a term causes smirks even today.

of haemorrhoids and five golden mice, for the same plague afflicted you and your five lords."[1] **The five lords of the Philistine cities protested to the people, "Are we to be made into laughing stocks before the Israelites! Are we to be compared to mice and haemorrhoids? Perhaps this is not a plague from the God of Israel." The priests and diviners replied, "It is the hand of the God of Israel. Unless you humiliate yourselves before him his anger will not abate.** You must make models of your haemorrhoids and the mice that are devastating the land to give honour to the God of Israel. Perhaps he will lighten his hand upon you, your gods and your land. Why do you harden your hearts just as Egypt and Pharaoh hardened their hearts? Only after he made fools of them, did they let Israel go."[2]

The priests and the diviners said to the lords of the Philistines: "This is how you will know that the plague comes from the LORD of Israel. Take wood and make one new cart with two nursing cows who have never borne a yoke. Harness the cows to the cart but take their calves who follow them to the barn; then take the Ark of the LORD, set it on the cart; put all the gold articles which you are giving to him as a guilt offering into a chest by its side; send it off and let it go. Then, if, without a driver, it goes up the border road by way of Beth-shemesh, **you will know** that it was he, **the Lord of Israel,** who afflicted us with this great evil. But if not, if the cows do not go, we shall know that it was not his hand that struck us and that it just happened to us by chance.

The people did so: they took two mothering cows, harnessed them to the cart and shut their calves indoors. They set the Ark of the LORD upon the cart along with the chest containing the gold mice

[1] A golden image of a haemorrhoid and rat for each of the lords of the five cities is too funny to be factual. The author is poking fun at the Philistine lords for the entertainment of his Judean audience.

[2] The suggestion here is that the lords of the Philistines, like Pharaoh, are not certain that the affliction comes from God or is a natural disaster.

and the image of their haemorrhoids. **In spite of the bleating of their calves calling after them**, the cows went straight ahead on the road – the way towards Beth-shemesh, keeping to the one road, mooing as they went, neither turning off to the right or left. The lords of the Philistines walked behind them even to the borders of Beth-shemesh. **The people of** Beth-shemesh were reaping the wheat harvest in the valley. They looked up and saw the Ark and were overjoyed to see it. When the cart reached the farm of Joshua of Beth-shemesh, it stopped. There, after splitting up the wood of the cart for fuel, they offered up the cows as a burnt offering to the LORD. The Levites had lowered the Ark of the LORD along with the chest with all the golden objects and set them on the stone. The people of Beth-shemesh offered up burnt offerings and other sacrifices to the LORD on that day. The five lords of the Philistines witnessed it and returned to Ekron that same day.

The people rejoiced when they saw the tribute of the Philistines: namely, the golden haemorrhoids that the Philistines offered up as a guilt offering to the LORD – one for Ashdod, one for Gaza, one for Ashkelon, one for Gath, one for Ekron; as for the golden mice, they were as many as the cities ruled by the five lords of the Philistines – both the fortified cities and open villages. Witness to this is the great stone upon which they rested the Ark of the LORD; to this very day it is in the fields of Joshua, of Beth-shemesh. **It is a memorial to what the Lord did to the people;** he struck down the men of Beth-shemesh because they peered into the Ark of the LORD **to see what it contained.** He struck down seventy men **but, because Beth-shemesh was small,** it was as if fifty thousand men had been slain. The people mourned because the LORD had brought such a great slaughter upon the town. The people of Beth-shemesh cried, "Who is able to stand before the LORD, this awesome God, and to whom shall he go up from us?" They sent messengers to the inhabitants of Kiryath-jearim to say, "The

Philistines have returned the Ark of the LORD; come down and take it for yourselves."

The men of Kiriath-jearim came and took the Ark of the LORD and brought it to the home of Abinadab on the hill. Eliezer, his son, was given the holy charge to keep guard over the Ark of the LORD. The Ark rested in Kiryath-jearim a long time – twenty years.

Samuel routes the Philistines

The Philistines ruled over Israel and exacted tribute from them. The Israelites did not go to sacrifice to the Lord because Kiriath-jearim was on the border of Philistia and they were frightened that they would be attacked. But the whole people of Israel longed for the LORD **because he had forsaken them for the Philistines.** So Samuel spoke to all the Israelites saying, "If you would return to the LORD with utter sincerity, you must remove the images of foreign gods from your homes as well as the Astartes. Direct your hearts to the LORD, to serve him alone. Then he will deliver you from the might of the Philistines." Then the Israelites removed the Baals and the Astartes.[1] They served the LORD alone.

Samuel commanded: "Gather all Israel to Mizpah. I will pray for your sake to the LORD." They assembled at Mizpah, drew water and made libations before the LORD. They fasted on that day and there declared, "We have sinned against the LORD." At Mizpah Samuel reigned as judge[2] over the Israelites.

---

[1] Baal and Astarte were the local male and female gods whose worship was thought to guarantee plentiful rainfall and harvests. The plural indicates that there were many images of these deities.

[2] The Judges of Israel are to be compared to chieftains, those who led their people into war and acted as chief magistrates. Samuel is a transitional figure. He is a Seer – a combination of judge and oracle, the ideal ruler because he rules as God's deputy.

The Philistines heard that the Israelites had assembled at Mizpah. The lords of the Philistines went up against Israel. When the Israelites heard this they were afraid of the Philistines. The Israelites implored Samuel, "Do not stop crying for help from the LORD our God, that he may save us from the hands of the Philistines." Samuel took one suckling lamb and offered it up as a whole burnt offering to the LORD. He cried to the LORD on behalf of Israel. The LORD heeded his plea. While Samuel was making his offering, the Philistines drew near to war against Israel. **This is how the Lord answered Samuel's petition:** The LORD thundered so loudly on that day against the Philistines that they panicked **and fled, leaving their weapons behind them.** Thus they were routed before the Israelites because the men of Israel went out from Mizpah in pursuit of the Philistines. **They picked up their fallen weapons** and struck them down until they came as far as the land below Beth-car.

Samuel ordered a large rock to be taken and put between Mizpah and Shen and named the place Eben-ezer for he said, "Until now the LORD has helped us."[1] The Philistines were humbled and no longer raided Israel's borders. The hand of the LORD was against the Philistines throughout the years of Samuel's rule over Israel. The cities which the Philistines had captured from Israel were restored to the Israelites from Ekron to Gath. Also the frontier towns on the border did Israel deliver from the rule of the Philistines. There was also peace between Israel and the indigenous Amorites. Samuel judged Israel all the days of his active life. Each year he made a circuit of Beth-el, Gilgal and Mizpah. He handed down judgements on the Israelites at those places. Then he returned to Ramah because his home was there. There also he judged the Israelites and he built an altar to the LORD.

When Samuel was old, he made his sons judges over Israel. Joel

---

[1] Eben means "rock" and Ezer means "help".

was the name of the firstborn, Abijah was the name of the second. They were judges **over the southern district** in Beersheba; **Samuel continued to judge in the cities of the north.** His sons did not follow his example; they pursued profit, they accepted bribes for which they perverted justice.

All the elders of Israel joined together and went to Samuel at Ramah. They said to him, "See now, you are growing old, your sons are not following in your footsteps. Now, therefore, appoint us a king to rule over us **so that we may be** like the other nations." Their words displeased Samuel **not because of his sons but** that they said, "Appoint for us a king to rule over us." Samuel prayed to the LORD **to know what to do.** The LORD answered Samuel, "Hear the people's voice, all they said to you: for they have not rejected you but they have rejected me from being king over them.[1] It is like all they have done since the day I brought them up out of Egypt until this very day. Just as they have forsaken me to serve other gods, they are behaving towards you. Now, do what they ask, but make certain to forewarn them – tell them of the customs of the kings who will rule over them."

Samuel conveyed all the words of the LORD to all the people who clamoured to him for a king. He said, "This will be the manner of the king who reigns over you, he will requisition your sons to be his charioteers and cavalry; they shall run before his chariots to give him honour. He will commission them as generals of thousands and captains of companies of fifty. **He will levy people** to plough the land, to reap his harvest, to make weapons of war and trappings for his chariots. He will abduct your daughters to be perfumers; to be cooks and to be bakers. He will expropriate your fields, your vineyards, your olive groves, the very best of

---

[1] The importance of this view of the monarchy has been overshadowed by the importance given to the kingdom of David who is the Messiah's ancestor. The fact is that the appointment of a king was in the prophetic view a compromise made by God with a rebellious people.

them, **not only for himself** but to give to his ministers. He will
tax a tenth of your seed and your vineyards to pay his officials
and his courtiers **and household staff.** He will seize your male
servants and your maids, your best young men and your donkeys
to work for him. Likewise, a tenth of your flocks; indeed, you will
all be his servants. On that day you will cry out because of the
king whom you yourselves chose. But God will not respond **to
your appeal** on that day."

But the people refused to listen to Samuel's warning: they shouted,
"No, but there shall be a king over us. We too will be like all the
nations **of the world.** Our king will be our judge. He will go out
before us to fight our battles **and come home victorious.**" Samuel
heard all that the people said. He repeated it into the ears of the
LORD. The LORD said to Samuel, "Do what they ask, appoint them
a king." So Samuel agreed and told the Israelites: "Go now every
man to his city **and his home.**"

There was a Benjamite named Kish ben Abiel ben Zeror ben
Bekorath ben Aphiah, a Benjaminite and a man of great sub-
stance. He had a son whose name was Saul, a beautiful young
man. There was no man among the Israelites handsomer than
he. He stood head and shoulders above everyone else. Once, the
donkeys belonging to Kish, Saul's father, went astray. Kish
instructed Saul, his son, "Take one of the hands with you and
go and look for the donkeys." He passed through the hills of
Ephraim and crossed through the district of Shalishah but could
not find them. They passed through the district of Shaalim. They
were not there. He traversed the whole territory of Benjamin but
could not find them. When they arrived at the district of Zuph,
Saul said to the lad with him, "We had better return, otherwise
my father will stop worrying about the donkeys and start worrying about us." He replied, "See, there is a man of God in this
town, a man highly honoured, whatever he predicts happens.
Now, let us go there. Maybe he can direct us to the way we

should go." "If we go," replied Saul, "what can we bring the man, seeing that there is no more food in our bags? There is no present to bring to the man of God. We have nothing with us!" The lad persisted in persuading Saul, "See, I have found with me a quarter of a silver shekel. I will give it to the man of God to tell us what road to take." [In Israel in olden days, when a person went for an answer from God, he would say, "Let us go to find the Seer", for he, who today is called a prophet, was in earlier times called a Seer.]

Saul agreed with his servant, "Well said, come, we will go." They went to the town where the man of God was. As they went uphill towards the town, they came upon young girls going out to draw water. They asked them, "Is the Seer in this place?" **Enchanted by Saul's beauty**, they answered **at great length**. "He is. He is before you. Go quickly now because he only today came to town, for the people today are sacrificing at the shrine. As you enter the town you will certainly find him, even before he goes up to the shrine to eat, because the people will not eat of the sacrifice until his arrival, because he must bless the sacrifice. Afterwards the guests may eat. Go up now, you will find him straightaway." They went up to the town. As they were entering the town, Samuel was going out to welcome them on his way to the shrine.

The LORD had revealed to Samuel the day before Saul's arrival: "Tomorrow, about this time, I will send to you a Benjaminite. You will anoint him as a prince over my people Israel. He will deliver my people from the hands of the Philistines, for I have seen the plight of my people because their cries of oppression have reached me." **For, now that Samuel had lost his authority over Israel, the Philistines once again raided and taxed the people of Israel.** When Samuel saw Saul, the LORD told him: "Behold – the man of whom I said, he is to govern my people." Saul approached Samuel within the gate, "Please tell me where is the Seer's house?" "I am the Seer," Samuel answered Saul. "Go up before me to the shrine. You will eat with me today. In the morning I will send you off but before then I will tell you everything that is in your heart **and mind to do." Before Saul could say a word, Samuel continued,** "As for the donkeys you have lost three days ago, do not be concerned over them. They have been found. **But they are of no matter compared to the question,** for whom does all Israel set its desire? Is it not for you and for your father's house? **Shall you not lead them into battle against the Philistines?"** Saul replied, "Am I not only a Benjaminite? I am from the smallest of the tribes of Israel and my family the least of all the families of the tribe of Benjamin. How can you speak to me in this fashion?" **Samuel replied, "My son, you have been chosen by the Lord. He sent you to me and told me that you would come. You will soon see what I have prepared for your coming."** Samuel took Saul and his servant to the dining room. He placed them at the head of some thirty guests. Samuel instructed the cook, "Bring the portion which I gave you and of which I said to you, 'Keep it by you.'" The cook lifted the meat of the thigh and placed it before Saul. Then did Samuel say: "See that which has been set aside has been placed before you. Eat, because it has been kept to await your appointed arrival along with the people I invited." So Saul did eat with Samuel on that day.

Samuel anoints Saul

When they came down from the shrine **to the town, they spread out bedding on the roof of Samuel's lodgings.** Samuel spoke to Saul on the housetop **about his future before both he and his servant went to sleep.** They rose early in the morning. At the break of day, Samuel called to Saul who was on the roof, "Rise up so that I may say goodbye to you." Saul got up and both of them, he and Samuel, went out into the street. As they were approaching the outskirts of the town, Samuel said to Saul, "Tell the lad to walk ahead of us [he walked ahead] but you stop here for a time so that I may tell you the will of God." **Samuel told Saul that the elders had asked for a king, to be like the other nations, and to fight the Philistines, and that God had chosen Saul to be his anointed one. In spite of all the wondrous events, Saul could not believe this: he was in his own eyes a simple man who had been sent out to find his father's donkeys, not to become king over the Lord's people, Israel.** Samuel took a vial of oil, poured it over his head, kissed him and said, "Has not the LORD anointed you as prince over his inheritance, Israel? You will govern the people of the LORD. You will deliver them from the hands of their enemies. These are the signs that the LORD has anointed you.[1]

"When you leave me you will find two men by the grave of Rachel, your ancestress, on the borders of the land of Benjamin. They will say to you, 'The donkeys you went looking for have been found.' **The very words you said to me about your father's concern**, they will say to you, 'Your father is no longer concerned for the donkeys but is worrying about you. He is saying, 'What shall I do about my missing son?' You will turn from there and go to the terebinth of Tabor. There you will find three men going up to God at Beth-el. One will be carrying three kids, the other three loaves of bread and another carrying a flask of wine. They will greet you, give you two loaves of bread which you will accept from them. After this, you will come to the mount of God **at Gibeah** where the officers of the Philistines are stationed. When you approach that town, you will meet an order of dervishes[2]

---

[1] The last three sentences are not in the Hebrew text but in the Septuagint and Vulgate, the ancient Greek and Roman translations.

[2] The Hebrew is "Neviim", plural of Navi, which is always translated as prophets. In view of the fact that the author previously has told us that Samuel was a prophet (Navi) who in 'those times was called a Seer (a See-er)' we can deduce that those whom we now consider as prophets were not the prophets to whom the author is referring. The fact, also, that they have all sorts of musical instruments indicates that they were more like chanting monks, seeking and spreading divine inspiration. I have, therefore, translated Niviim as dervishes.

coming down from the shrine with lyres, timbrels, flutes and harps. They will be in an ecstatic state – **singing, chanting and dancing.** The spirit of the LORD will mightily come upon you. You will join in the ecstasy and turn into another man. When these signs are fulfilled, act as you will because the divine spirit will be with you. However, **when you are king** you will go down before me to Gilgal **to muster up your forces to fight against the Philistines.** There I will meet you to offer up burnt offerings and to sacrifice peace offerings on behalf of Israel. Seven days you must wait until I come to you and tell you what you must do **to remove the Philistine yoke."** Saul said to Samuel, "You are a man of God, I revere you, but I do not wish to be king over Israel."

But, when he turned his back to depart from Samuel, God changed his nature. All the promised signs were fulfilled that same day: **two men by the tomb of Rachel told him that the donkeys were found and of his father's anxiety over his own safety, and three men by the terebinth of Tabor carrying kids, bread and wine. They gave him two loaves of bread as Samuel had said.** And, when they came to the mount of **Gibeah**[1], **he was amazed** an order of dervishes came to welcome him. A divine spirit overwhelmed him and he went into a frenzy with them. When all who knew him saw him chanting ecstatically together with the dervishes, they exclaimed to one another, "What has happened to the son of Kish – is Saul also among the dervishes?" A townsman asked, "But who is at their head?" **For the group had never been seen there before.** It is for this reason that we hear the expression to this very day, "Is Saul also among the dervishes?"[2]

When he finished his ecstatic chanting and dancing, he went to the heights of the town. Saul's uncle **greeted him and** asked him

---

[1] Saul's home.
[2] Obviously, an expression to indicate surprise at an individual's change in position and status.

and the servant, "Where did you go? **Your father was so worried.**" He replied, "**You know we went** to seek the donkeys. When we could not find them, we enquired of Samuel. Saul's uncle **was very surprised to hear of his meeting Samuel, he** asked him, "Please tell me, what did Samuel say to you?" Saul answered his uncle, "He told us that the donkeys were found." But he said nothing of what Samuel had said about the kingship.

Samuel then summoned all the people to the LORD at Mizpah. He criticized the people of Israel, "This is what the LORD, the God of Israel, says, 'I brought Israel out of Egypt, I rescued you from the hands of the Egyptians and from all the kingdoms who were oppressing you. But you, now, have despised and rejected your God – he who saved you from all your trials and tribulations. Nonetheless you say to him, "No, but set a king over us!" This being so, stand before the LORD according to your tribes, your clans and families **to see whom he will choose to be your king.**"

Thus did Samuel bring forward the leaders of the tribes of Israel. **Lots were taken** and it fell upon the tribe of Benjamin. So the heads of the clans of the tribe of Benjamin came forward. **Lots were taken** and it fell upon the family of the Matrites. **Lots were taken of all the adults of the Matrites** and it finally fell upon Saul the son of Kish. **But Saul who knew that it would be his lot to be king hid, for he did not wish to rule over Israel in God's place.** So, when they looked for him, he could not be found. Again they asked[1] of the LORD, "Has the man been here?" The LORD answered: "See, he is hiding among the luggage." So they ran and took him from there. When he took his place among the people he was a head taller than any of them.

---

[1] The three-letter root of the verb to ask; *sh-a-l*, are the same three letters of *Sh-a-ul*, Saul's Hebrew name. The symbolism of his name is further attested when Samuel will again condemn Israel for "asking" for a king. The "asked for" king is named 'he who was asked for'. This could suggest that Saul was more of a literary/legendary figure than an historic personality.

Samuel declared to the entire people, "Have you seen whom the LORD has chosen? There is none like him among all the people." The whole crowd cried out: "Long live the king." Samuel explained to the people the rules of the kingdom. He also wrote it on a scroll and placed it before the LORD.

But Saul did not agree to be king, he felt unworthy of the task. He said, "Let the Lord rule over us. Samuel will be our judge. He will lead us into war against our enemies." So Samuel dismissed the people, every person to his own home. Saul also went to his home to Gibeah. There went with him **a guard of honour –** valiant men whom God had inspired. But there were certain troublemakers who said **aloud,** "How can this man save us **from our enemies?"** For they despised him and offered him no present. But he, **Saul, did not protest but** held his peace.

Not long after this, Nahash the Ammonite rose up and laid siege against Jabesh-gilead **east of Mount Gilboa.** All the men of Jabesh said to Nahash, "Make a treaty with us and we will be your subjects." Nahash the Ammonite replied to them, "On this condition I will enter into a treaty with you, that I gouge out everyone's right eye and thus humiliate the whole of Israel." The elders of Jabesh pleaded with him, "Allow us seven days' grace. **If we agree to your condition and save our lives all Israel will be disgraced by our action.** Let us send messengers throughout the borders of Israel, **to tell the tribes of Israel what you propose to do.** If then no one comes to our rescue, we will surrender to you." **Nahash agreed, "The Israelites will not come up against me."**

The messengers came to Gibeah, where Saul lived. They recounted these events to the townsfolk. All of them raised their voices and cried aloud. Just then, Saul was coming out of the fields driving his cattle. Saul asked, "What is wrong? Why are the people crying?" And they told him of the words of the men from Jabesh. When he heard these things, he was seized with great fury for the spirit of God had taken hold of him. He took a yoke of oxen, cut them into pieces, and sent them throughout all the borders of Israel in the hands of the messengers with these instructions, "Those who do not join Saul and Samuel, so will be done to their cattle!" **For Saul saw that he had to save Jabesh-gilead and not bring disgrace upon the people of Israel.**

The fear of the LORD came upon the whole people and they assembled for war as one man. He mustered them at Bezek, **a day's march from Jabesh.** The sons of Israel were three hundred thousand and those of Judah thirty thousand. The messengers who had come **from Jabesh** were told: "Thus shall you say to the men of Jabesh-gilead, 'Tomorrow, by the time the sun is hot, you will be saved.'" The messengers returned and reported this to the men of Jabesh-gilead and they were jubilant. **To put Nahash off his guard,** the men of Jabesh said, "Tomorrow we will come out to you, you may do to us whatsoever pleases you."

So it was that, on the next day, Saul divided his forces into three divisions. They came into the midst of the **Ammonite** camp during the morning watch and struck the Ammonites until the heat of the day. Those that remained **alive** were scattered, so that **of all the Ammonite army** two were not left together. **So grateful were the people of Israel for their victory, that** the people said to Samuel, "Who is it that said, 'Will Saul rule over us?' Hand over to us these men so that we may kill them." But Saul intervened, "No man will be put to death this day for this is the day that the LORD has wrought a great deliverance in Israel."

Samuel declared to the people, "Let us go to Gilgal and confirm there the kingdom of Saul." The entire people proceeded to Gilgal and crowned Saul king before the LORD at Gilgal and sacrificed peace offerings before the LORD. There did Saul and all the men of Israel celebrate with great rejoicing.

Samuel's farewell address

And Samuel said to all Israel, "You see that I have paid attention
to all that you said to me and have appointed a king to rule over
you. See the king will now be your ruler. And I am grown old
and grey; my sons are no younger than you, but I have ruled
over you from my youth until now. Here I am: Let anyone give
evidence against me before the LORD and before his anointed king,
whose ox have I taken, whose donkey have I taken, whom have
I defrauded, whom have I oppressed, at whose hand have I
accepted a bribe to blind my eyes? **Tell me** and I will make recompense to you!" They answered **as one man**: "You have not
defrauded us nor have you oppressed us, you have taken nothing
from anyone." He then said to them, "The LORD is witness against
you, and his anointed is witness against you today, that you have
found nothing wrong in my behaviour." They answered: "They
are witness **to what you have said**."

Then Samuel proceeded to say to the people, "It was the LORD
who appointed Moses and Aaron and who brought your ancestors
up from the land of Egypt. Now, stand silently and I shall enter
with you in judgement on behalf of the LORD to prove how righteously did the LORD deal with you and your ancestors. When
the **house** of Jacob had come down to Egypt, **and Pharaoh and
the Egyptians made them do hard labour;** then our ancestors
cried out to the LORD and the LORD sent Moses and Aaron who
brought your ancestors out of Egypt and he settled them in this
land. But they forgot the LORD their God and he handed them
over into the hand of Sisera, commander of Hazor's[1] army and
into the hands of the Philistines and the king of Moab and they
were in constant battle with them. And they cried out to the
LORD, saying, 'We have sinned because we have forsaken the

---

[1] Hazor was the capital of Jabin, king of the Canaanites.

LORD and worshipped Baalim and Ashtaroth;[1] now save us from the hands of our enemies and we will serve only you.' So the LORD sent Jerubbaal and Bedan and Jephthah and Samuel[2] and delivered you from the power of your enemies who surrounded you and you then lived in security. And when you saw that Nahash the king of the Ammonites was preparing to attack you, you said to me, **despite my protest,** 'No, we will have a king over us," when the LORD your God is your king! Now, therefore, here is the king that you have chosen, and whom you have asked for: so see the LORD has put a king over you, but if you fear the LORD and listen to his voice and rebel not against the LORD's word – **it will be well but only** if both you and the king who rules over you follow the LORD your God **to keep his laws.** But, if you do not heed the LORD's voice and you rebel against the word of the LORD, the power of the LORD will be against you and your king. Now, therefore, stand silently and behold this great miracle which the LORD will perform before your very eyes. Is it not the time of the wheat harvest **when no rain falls?** I will call upon the LORD for him to send thunder and rain; so that you may know how great is your wickedness – God does not approve your petition for an **earthly** king."

So Samuel called upon the LORD and the LORD sent thunder and rain that day and all the people greatly feared the LORD and Samuel **because of the miracle.** The people pleaded with Samuel, "Pray for your servants to the LORD your God that we do not die, for in addition to all our existing sins, we have added this evil to ask for a king to rule over us."

Samuel reassured the people, "Do not be frightened. While you have indeed done this evil thing, you need not turn away from

---

[1] Male and female fertility deities of Canaan.

[2] Jerubbaal (also known as Gideon) and Jephthah are two tribal chieftains recorded in the book of Judges. Bedan is not recorded. Samuel's reference to himself in the third person is of interest.

obeying the LORD, but you should serve the LORD with all your heart. Do not turn away **from him** – to worship false gods which cannot profit you or deliver you for they are utterly useless. **If you are faithful to the Lord your God even though you have chosen a human king to rule over you**, the LORD will not forsake his people **if only** to preserve his own honour in that it has pleased the LORD to make you his own people. And, as for me, perish the thought that I should sin against the LORD by ceasing to pray on your behalf. And I will continue to lead you in the proper paths. Only respect the LORD and serve him loyally with all your heart for remember his greatness in dealing with you, but if you continue in your wickedness both you and your king **with you** will be swept away.

Saul was **thirty-**one years old when he became king and he reigned for **twenty-**two years over Israel[1]. Saul picked three thousand men from Israel **to be his standing army.** Two thousand were stationed with Jonathan, **his son,** in Gibeath-benjamin. The rest of his army he sent away – each man to his home.

---

[1] According to the Hebrew text, Saul was one year old when he became king and reigned for two years. The impossibility of this led to this verse being dropped from the Septuagint. I follow in part the Revised English Bible which employs some Greek Manuscripts which say 'thirty' when he began his reign. The Jewish Roman historian Josephus says he ruled for twenty years. I am intrigued by the inclusion of this verse in the Hebrew text. Is the author telling us that the whole life of Saul is make-believe – a fable about a person who did not want to be a king and a prophet-seer who also did not want a king, but had no choice for he had to bend to the will of the people? The unfolding of the tale indicates that, while Samuel anointed him as king, he insists that he must act under his instructions, and when he does not, he is told that his kingdom will not pass on to his children. The king will only become the supreme ruler when Samuel dies. The fact that Saul means in Hebrew 'The asked for [king]' and that, even on his anointment as king, Samuel attacks the people for 'asking' for a king could suggest that the whole history of Saul is a parable to articulate the opposition of the Hebrew prophets to the monarchy because according to their theology attested to in Deuteronomy as well as in the Books of Samuel, only Yahweh (the LORD) should be king over his chosen people.

Now Jonathan struck **and wiped out** the Philistine garrison in Geba. When the Philistines heard of it, **they** mobilised **to take revenge.**

Saul had trumpets blown by messengers throughout the land, crying out, "Let the Hebrews hear, **not only the Israelites, but our neighbours who like us have been subjects of the Philistines for too long. We have destroyed the Philistine garrison at Geba. Come to me and let us rid ourselves of the Philistine yoke over us."** So all of Israel heard that Saul had struck a Philistine garrison and had enraged the Philistines against Israel. The people rallied around Saul in Gilgal.

But then the Philistines mobilised themselves to do battle against Israel – thirty thousand chariots **with their charioteers,** and a cavalry of six thousand horsemen, and soldiers as numerous as the sand on the seashore. And, when they had come up to camp at Michmas, east of Beth-aven, the men of Israel realised that they were in dire straits for the people were terrified **of the vengeance of the Philistines.** They hid in caves and behind thickets, between boulders, in caverns and wells. Many of the Hebrews crossed the Jordan to find refuge in the lands of Gad and Gilead. Saul, however, **and his army** were still in Gilgal but all the forces with him were very agitated. He delayed taking action for seven days as Samuel had instructed **him when they had first met and he had been anointed to be prince over Israel,** but Samuel did not arrive and the people began to disperse, deserting him **because, if there was to be no battle, they would return home to look after their families.** Saul, realising this, said, "Bring me the burnt and peace offerings **so that we may sacrifice to the Lord before we go into battle."** And he sacrificed the burnt offering. Just as he had concluded sacrificing the burnt offering, look Samuel came. Saul went to greet him to show respect, but he demanded of him, "What have you done? **You were instructed to await my instructions."** Saul defended himself, "When I saw the men deserting me, and you had not come at the agreed time – the Philistines having mustered at Michmas – I thought, the Philistines will descend upon me at Gilgal, without my even entreating the LORD's favour. I had **no choice much as I did not want but** to offer up the burnt offering. **That is why I did not wait for you."** Samuel replied, "You have acted foolishly, you have not kept the commandment of the LORD which he commanded you **through my mouth. Had you had faith and waited for my coming,** the LORD would have fixed your kingdom over Israel forever.

Saul's kingdom will not endure

"But now your kingdom will not endure. The LORD is looking for a man after his own heart. The LORD has already decided whom to appoint to be prince over his people, because you did not keep that which the LORD had commanded you.

Saul repressed his anger, thinking: "This is grievously unjust, I never asked to be king. I was content to be a commoner. I resisted Samuel's call to be king. I hid when chosen. Only when the people called on me to deliver them, and I routed their enemies and they asked me to become king, did I accept the anointment from Samuel's hand. Now that I am king and because I acted as a king – is the kingdom to be wrestled away from me?"

Saul protested to Samuel, "Why have you done this to me? Why did you not come within the seven days? The people were waiting for your sacrifice and blessing O man of God. When you did not come they believed that you had forsaken them because they wanted a king and had rejected the Lord and you, his prophet-priest. Did you not promise at this very place that you would pray to the Lord to save us from our enemies. Why do you betray your people? Did you not tell me that God had chosen me? Why should I be punished for the people's rebelliousness? How can I

fight the battles of the Lord if you are not with me?" But Samuel was silent and turned his back to him.[1]

Samuel went his way from Gilgal to Gibeath-benjamin. When Saul numbered the men remaining with him there were only about six hundred. Saul and Jonathan his son and those men with him were encamped in Geba in the land of Benjamin, and the Philistines encamped at Michmas. Three companies of raiders came out of the Philistine camp. One company made for Ophrah in the district of Shaul. One made for Beth-horon, and one made for the border road that overlooks the valley of Zeboim on the way to the desert.

Now, **at that time** there was not a single blacksmith in all of Israel, for the Philistines had thought that the Hebrews would **employ them to** make swords and spears. **The Philistines had during their rule forbidden blacksmithing and the skills of the smith had been forgotten.** Thus, all the Israelites had to go to the Philistines – every one of them – to sharpen their ploughshares, matlocks for turning over ground, axes and sickles. The **oppressive** charge was a pim[2] for sharpening ploughshares, matlocks, three-pronged forks, axes and for setting the goads. So, at the time of war, neither sword nor spear could be found in the hand of any Israelite who was with Saul and Jonathan. Only they were armed with them. **But the men carried slings, bows, staves, axes and forks.**

The garrison of Philistines marched out to the pass of Michmas **from which cliff they could see the Israelite camp across the valley.** One day, Jonathan said to his arms-bearer, "Come, let us go across to the Philistine garrison on the other side." But he did

---

[1] My intervention is due to the ambivalence of Samuel towards Saul who seems to be the scapegoat of the prophet's anger for the people's rejection of God and the prophet as his sole deputy to rule over them.

[2] About a gram of silver.

not inform his father **of this perilous adventure.** Saul was staying in the outskirts of Gibeah under the pomegranate tree in Migron and the forces with him were some six hundred men.

Now the people with Saul also did not know of Jonathan's departure. Flanking the ravine, which Jonathan was seeking to cross to reach the Philistine garrison, were rocky crags on both sides. One was called Bozez and the other Seneh, one of them was to the north towards Michmas, the other one to the south towards Geba. Now Jonathan said to his arms-bearer, "Come, let us cross over to that outpost of the uncircumcised. Perhaps the LORD will act on our behalf for in regard to the LORD's **power to** deliver, it is of no consequence whether we are many or few." His arms-bearer replied to him, "Act according to your desire. Go to; I am with you all the way." Jonathan said, "In that case, when we reach the men, we will let them see us. Now, if they say to us, 'Stay until we come to you,' we will remain where we are and not go up to them, but if they say, 'Come up to us,' we will go up for it means that the LORD has given them into our grasp. That will be the sign." The two of them revealed themselves to the Philistine outpost and the Philistines called out, "See, the Hebrews are crawling out of the holes where they are hiding." The men of the outpost called to Jonathan and his arms-bearer, "Come up to us and we will teach you a thing **or two.**" Jonathan said to his arms-bearer, "Follow after me for the LORD has given them into the hand of Israel!" He climbed up on his hands and feet – his arms-bearer after him. They fell before Jonathan's **attack** and his arms-bearer was finishing them off after him. In that first onslaught of Jonathan's and his arms-bearer they slew some twenty soldiers – **like men** cutting in a furrow within an acre of land. Terror struck both in and out of the camp – the whole army both in the garrison and the raiding parties were shaking **with fear.** The very earth shook **as if it were** an earthquake sent from God.

Saul's look-out men in Gibeah of Benjamin could see the men were scattering – running aimlessly in every direction. **Saul could not understand the cause of the rout of the Philistines.** Saul said to his forces, "Call the roll to see who has gone from us." They called the roll – Jonathan and his arms-bearer were missing. (The **Ephod**[1] was being worn by Ahijah ben Ahitub, **that is** Ichabod's brother, the son of Phinehas ben Eli who, **as you will remember,** was the priest of the LORD in Shiloh.)[2] And Saul said to Ahijah, "Bring forward the Ephod [for he was the man who was wearing the Ephod in Israel at that time]." But even while Saul was speaking to the priest the tumult in the Philistine camp was ever increasing. **Saul decided that there was no need to enquire of the Lord; he would engage the Philistines in battle.** Saul said to the priest: "Desist from consulting the oracle." Saul and all his forces mustered themselves and came to the battle. **They found the Philistines in great panic,** their swords were directed against each other in great confusion. Those Hebrews[3] that had been earlier conscripted by the Philistines and had joined them in the camp **to fight against Israel,** they too deserted to fight alongside Israel with Saul and Jonathan. When all the men of Israel who were hiding in the hills of Ephraim heard that the Philistines were fleeing, they too joined in battle to pursue them. So the LORD delivered Israel on that day. The battle ground moved forward to Beth-aven.

The army of Israel were that day exhausted **through hunger,** but Saul, **exhilarated by the victory,** put a ban on the army: "Cursed be the man who eats food before evening until I am avenged on my enemies." So none of the army so much as tasted any food.

---

[1] The breastplate worn by the High Priest containing twelve stones which allegedly sparkled in response to questions directed to God to discover his will.
[2] The bracketed sentence is I Samuel 14:3 which I have moved here before 14:18 because it seems to be a more appropriate place for it.
[3] The use of Hebrews here indicates that they were not, as commonly thought, the Israelites but a grouping of peoples who included the tribes of Israel.

The whole army came upon honeycombs and honey was on the ground. When the troops came upon the honeycomb the honey was dripping but none put out his hand to take the honey to his mouth because they respected the ban **of Saul against eating**. Jonathan, however, was not present when his father had put this ban upon the army. He extended the end of the staff which he held to dip it into the honeycomb and raised it to his mouth. The taste brightened his eyes which had been dulled by hunger. One of the soldiers protested; "Your father severely charged us with this oath: 'Cursed be the man who eats food this day.' All of us are faint from hunger." Jonathan retorted, "My father has imposed an unnecessary hardship upon the people. Consider how my eyes have brightened because of a taste of honey. How much greater would the slaughter of the Philistines have been had they eaten freely of the spoils left by their enemies."

On that day they slew the Philistines between Michmas and Aijalon. Because the men were aching with hunger, they flew upon the spoil; they seized sheep, oxen and calves and slew them on the ground and ate them with their blood. They reported this to Saul, "See, the people are sinning against the LORD in that they are eating meat with blood in it." Saul scolded them, "You have been rebellious; now roll a great stone before me." Saul ordered them, "Scatter yourselves among the troops and instruct them, 'Let every man bring me his ox or sheep and slay them here on this rock and then eat and not sin against the LORD by eating raw meat with blood in it.'" That night everyone brought his ox and slew them there. Saul bult an altar to the LORD. That was the first altar he ever built to the LORD.

Then Saul said, "Let us go down to the Philistines tonight and plunder them until the morning light. Let us not spare any of them." His men replied: "Do what you think is best." But the priest intervened, "Let us approach the divine oracle." So Saul enquired of God: "Shall I go down after the Philistines, will you deliver them into the power of the Israelites?" But he did not answer him at that time. Saul commanded, "Come here to me – all you chiefs of this people – to learn what sin has been committed today and why the LORD our God will not tell us what to do. Now as the LORD lives, he who delivers Israel, even if it be my son Jonathan, he will surely die."

Not one among the whole assembly answered him, **though some knew that Jonathan had not kept the ban against eating.** He said to all of the Israelites, "You shall be on one side. I and Jonathan my son will be on the other side. **God through the sacred lots will tell us who is guilty.** And the people said to Saul, "Do what you think is best." Then Saul petitioned the LORD, the God of Israel, "Why did you not answer your servant today? LORD, God of Israel, if the guilt lies with me or Jonathan my son, let the lot be *Urim*. If it is your people Israel, let the lot be *Thummin*." The lot fell on Saul and Jonathan.[1] So the people were exonerated. Then Saul said, "Cast the lot between me and Jonathan, my son." The lot fell on Jonathan. Saul said to Jonathan, "Tell me, what have you done?" And Jonathan told him saying, "I most certainly did taste some honey using the end of the staff which was in my hand. Here I am. I will die **for breaking your ban.**" Saul said, "Thus God will do to me and even worse, **if I release you because you are my beloved son.** You must surely die, Jonathan." But the people said to Saul: "Shall Jonathan die! He who wrought this great salvation for Israel? This cannot be, as the LORD lives, not one of the hairs of his head will fall to the ground, for he has

---

[1] The question asked of God by Saul and the method of determining the guilty party is not in the Hebrew text but in the Septuagint, the ancient Greek translation. There is speculation about the Urim and Thummin. What were they? All agree that it was part of the breastplate worn by the High Priest. Were they two lots which could indicate a simple yes or no? The Jewish tradition is that they were twelve precious or semi-precious stones in four columns which would sparkle to give a more complicated answer according to a known code.

wrought **our salvation** with God on this day." Thus did the people rescue Jonathan from death. **Saul listened to the people and held back his hand from slaying his son, but** Saul **lost heart and** gave up his intention and did not pursue the Philistines, so they returned to their homes.

Saul established his kingdom over Israel by waging successful wars against all his enemies on all his borders, against Moab, against the Ammonites and against Edom and against the kings of Zobah and against the Philistines. Whomever he turned against came off worse. He fought valiantly. He defeated the Amalekites. He delivered Israel out of the hands of their former raiders. [The sons of Saul were Jonathan, Ishvi and Malchishua, the names of his two daughters: the elder was Merab, the younger Michal, the name of Saul's wife was Ahinoam the daughter of Ahimaaz. The name of his commander-in-chief was Abner, ben Ner, Saul's uncle. Both Kish, Saul's father, and Ner, Abner's father, were sons of Abiel.] The warring against the Philistines was constant throughout Saul's life. Wherever Saul discovered any strong or brave man, he drafted him into his service.

Samuel was surprised at Saul's victories against his enemies for he had not waited for him to make the sacrifices but had made his own offerings to the Lord at Gilgal. Samuel was angry that the Lord was with Saul and that he the Lord's prophet had been rejected by the people. Samuel said, "I will test Saul to prove his unworthiness." So Samuel went up to Saul and made peace with him.

The war against Amalek

Samuel said to Saul, "**Remember that** it was me whom the LORD sent to anoint you to be king over his people, Israel. Now therefore listen to the command of the LORD. Thus says the LORD of hosts, "I remember **now** what Amalek did to Israel, how he attacked them on the road, on their way up from Egypt. **I said to Moses that I will utterly blot out any remembrance of Amalek from under the sky, and Moses built an altar to me and called it the 'Lord is my banner' because he said that as Amalek's hand was against his people, Israel, the Lord will be at war with Amalek for all time.**[1] Now go and destroy Amalek and execute the curse of destruction on all he has. Do not spare him, but kill men and women, infants and sucklings, oxen and sheep, camels and donkeys."

Saul summoned the people and reviewed them at Telaim. Two hundred thousand foot soldiers, ten thousand Judeans. Saul advanced against the city of the Amalekites and waited in ambush by the river-bed in the valley. Saul ordered the Kenites, "Get yourself away from the Amalekites lest I wipe you away with them, for you were kind to all the Israelites when they came up from Egypt." So the Kenites withdrew from among the Amalekites. Saul crushed the Amalekites from Havilah on the way to Shur, which is by Egypt. He took Agag, the king of the Amelekites, alive but, for all the people, he executed the ban by the sword. So Saul and the army spared Agag and the best of the sheep, the oxen, the fatlings, the lambs and all that was good. For they did not want to execute the curse of destruction except against that which was cheap and worthless. These they executed and destroyed.

The word of the LORD came to Samuel, "I regret appointing Saul king, for he has turned away from me; he has not executed my commands." **"O Lord, it was I who put him to the test to make him sin. I knew that he would not execute the curse against**

---

[1] My addition is a paraphrase of Exodus 15:14–16. The divine order to exterminate a people is what turns civilised people against religion. The only rationalization is that the curse was originally meant to be symbolic – the uprooting of all evil, for which reason the Israelites are not to make any profit out of the wholesale slaughter.

Amalek. Must I tell him that he has lost the kingdom forever?"
The Lord said to him: "You told him this when you had no cause,
when you did not go to Gilgal as you said you would. He did not
sin against me then when he offered up burnt offerings to me
before he went to fight the Philistines. But you were jealous for
your own glory as my prophet-priest. But now he has done wrong
in my sight. He has killed the men and women, infants and
sucklings, but he has spared the good oxen and sheep as spoil
for Israel and has taken alive the king of Amalek for his own
glory. So now go, tell him: his sons will not reign after him."

Samuel woke up early in the morning to visit Saul. Samuel was
told that Saul had reached Carmel. There he was setting up a
monument **to commemorate the victory over Amalek.** But he
had turned around and had left **Carmel** and gone down to Gilgal.
Samuel came upon Saul who said to him, "The LORD bless you.
I have fulfilled the LORD's command." Samuel asked, "What then
is the bleating of sheep in my ears and the lowing of oxen which
I can hear?" Saul replied, "They have brought them from the
Amalekites, the army spared the best of the sheep and oxen to
sacrifice to the LORD your God, all else has been destroyed." Then
Samuel silenced Saul, "Stop, and I will tell you what the LORD
said to me last night." He replied, "Speak." Samuel said, "You
may be small in your own sight but you are the head of the tribes
of Israel. The LORD anointed you king over Israel, he sent you on
a mission ordering you to execute the curse against the sinners
of Amalek, to war against them until they were finished off. Why
did you not listen to God's command? But you flew upon the
spoil, you did evil in the sight of God." Saul remonstrated with
Samuel, "But I have obeyed the word of the LORD and have done
as he ordered me. I have captured Agag, the king of the Amalekites, and have executed the divine ban of destruction upon all the
Amalekites. The army took of the spoil, sheep and oxen, the
choicest of the objects under the divine ban but only to offer
sacrifices to the LORD your God at Gilgal."

But Samuel retorted: "Does the LORD take pleasure in burnt offerings and sacrifices or in his people obeying his commands? Realize to obey is better than sacrifice, to listen is preferable to the fat of sacrificial rams, for the sin of rebellion is like that of divination. **Both reject the sovereignty of the** LORD, so too is arrogance like the iniquity of consulting idols **to determine the future.** Because you rejected the command of the LORD, he has rejected you as king of Israel."

Saul confessed to Samuel, "I have sinned because I have transgressed the LORD's command, and your own orders, because I was timid before the troops; I heeded their demands. But now, please forgive my sin. Come back with me and let me worship the LORD with you." But Samuel refused Saul's request, "I will not go back with you because, as I have said, you have rejected the LORD's command, so he has rejected you as king over Israel." As Samuel turned to go away, he took hold of the hem of his robe so that it tore. Samuel said to him, **"This is a sign.** The LORD has torn away the kingdom of Israel from you this day and has granted it to a man worthier than you. **Think not that you can appease the** LORD; the Glory of Israel does not deceive or change his mind as do humans."

He pleaded, "I accept that I have sinned, but please show me some respect before the elders of my people, and before Israel. Come back with me, so that with you I may offer obeisance to the LORD your God." **Samuel could not bear to see Saul's anguish,** so Samuel followed Saul, and Saul worshipped the LORD. Then Samuel gave an order, "Bring me Agag, king of Amalek!" Agag approached him, stumbling **as he went.** Agag spoke, "So now, bitter death is near." Samuel replied, "As your sword made women childless so your mother will become childless." So Samuel struck Agag down before the LORD at Gilgal. Samuel returned to Ramah and Saul went up to his house, at Gibeathshaul. Samuel never saw Saul again even to the day of his death;

and Samuel mourned for Saul and the LORD regretted making
Saul king over Israel.

David is anointed as Saul's successor

The LORD said to Samuel, "How long will you mourn over Saul,
when I have rejected him as king over Israel? Fill your horn with
oil and go. I am sending you to Jesse, the Bethlehemite, for I have
decided that one of his sons is to be king." But Samuel asked,
"How am I to go? If Saul hears **what I have done**, he will kill
me." The LORD replied, "Take a heifer with you and say, 'I am
come to sacrifice to the LORD.' Call Jesse to the sacrifice, then I
will tell you what to do and you will anoint for me the one I
point out to you." And Samuel did as the LORD had spoken and
came to Behtlehem. The elders of the city trembled as they went
out to meet him. **What had they done to bring God's prophet to
their village!** They asked, "Do you come with words of peace?"
He replied, "Yes, on an errand of peace. I have come to sacrifice
to the LORD. Purify yourselves and join me in the sacrificial meal."
He supervised the purification of Jesse and his sons and called
them to the sacrificial meal. When they arrived and he saw Eliab,
he thought, "Surely he is the LORD's anointed." But the LORD
chided Samuel, "Look not on at his appearance – his tall stature,
for I have rejected him. The LORD does not see as do men, for
they look at appearances but the LORD looks into the heart." Then
Jesse introduced Abinadab and made him pass before Samuel. He
thought, "Neither has the LORD chosen him." Jesse introduced
Shammah. He thought, "He too has not been chosen." And Jesse
made seven of his sons pass before Samuel, but Samuel said, "The
LORD has not chosen them." Samuel asked Jesse, "Are all your
children here?" He replied, "There is still the youngest, but he is
minding the sheep." Samuel commanded Jesse, "Send and fetch
him, for we will not sit down to eat **the sacrificial meal** until he
arrives here." So he sent for him and he was brought in. He was

ruddy in complexion with bright eyes and good looking. Then the LORD said; "Arise, anoint him for he is the one." Samuel took the horn of oil and anointed him amongst his brothers. The spirit of the LORD rested upon David from that day onwards. **Samuel commanded Jesse and his sons not to tell anyone how David was anointed by Samuel to be king over Israel for if Saul heard he would smite them and all of Bethlehem. Samuel, Jesse and his sons joined the elders of Bethlehem and sacrificed to the Lord and sat and ate together. His mission accomplished,** Samuel arose and returned to Ramah.

As the spirit of the LORD **had descended on David it** departed from Saul and an evil spirit from the LORD threw him into terror. Saul's servants told him, "An evil spirit from God is the cause of your terror. Let our lord now command your servants to look for a man skilled in playing the lyre so that when the divine evil spirit takes control of you, his hands will play for you and you will feel relief." Saul agreed with his servants, "Please find for me a man who plays well and bring him to me." One of the serving lads came forward, "I know a son of Jesse of Bethlehem who plays skilfully (also a powerful fellow, a warrior, worldly wise, a handsome man and the LORD is with him)."

Saul sent messengers to Jesse with the instructions, "Send to me David your son who minds the sheep." **Jesse was terrified for he remembered what Samuel had said. Had Saul heard of his anointment and had he sent for him to kill him; he asked the men, "Why does Saul want my son?" They replied, "An evil spirit from God has come over our lord and he has heard that David is skilful with his hands; he will play his lyre for him and the evil spirit will depart."** So Jesse loaded a donkey with bread, a skin of wine and a kid and sent them with David his son to give as a present to Saul. When David came to Saul and served him, he loved him very much. **So much so that** he became his arms-bearer. Saul sent Jesse this message: "Let David remain in my service for I like him." Whenever an evil spirit from God over-whelmed Saul, David fetched his lyre and struck its strings. Saul found relief. He felt better and the evil spirit left him.

The Philistines assembled their armies for war. They assembled together at Socoh in the territory of Judah. They encamped between Socoh and Azekah at Ephes-dammim. Saul and the forces of Israel were mustered and encamped in the valley of Elah where they drew up for battle against the Philistines. They were sta-tioned on one hill and Israel on the opposite hill and the valley separated them. A champion fighter came out from the Philistine camp. Goliath was his name, of the city of Gath. He was nine feet six inches tall. A bronze helmet covered his head. He was armed with a coat of mail. The weight of the coat was five thou-sand shekels of bronze.[1] He had bronze greaves on his legs, a bronze scimitar slung across his shoulders. The shaft of his javelin was shaped like a weavers beam, its head made of iron weighed six hundred shekels.[2]

A man carrying his shield walked before him. He stood and bellowed across to the armies of Israel these words, "Why do you come out to engage in battle? Am I not a Philistine and are you not Saul's soldiers? Pick a man to come down to me. If he can take me on in battle and strikes me down, we will be your servants but if I win and strike him down, you will be our servants and you will serve us." The Philistine said more, "I defy the armies of Israel today – provide for me a man and let us do battle together." Saul and all of Israel heard these words of the Philistine, they despaired and were terrified , **for they thought: "We have none as strong as this giant. When we engage the Philistines, how many more are there like him? How can we defeat them?"**

Now David was the son of the man from the family of Ephrath

[1] 220 pounds
[2] 30 pounds

of Bethlehem whose name is Jesse who had eight sons. The man, during Saul's reign, was old, aged beyond an ordinary lifespan. His three eldest sons had left and gone to Saul to the war. **Jesse asked the king to send David home as he was very old, and his three sons,** Eliab, the first born, the next eldest, Abinadab, and the third Shammah had gone to battle. **Saul agreed to let David go home on leave from time to time,** as David was the youngest and the three eldest had joined Saul. So David **came home, but** would go back and forth from Saul to shepherd his father's flock at Bethlehem.

The Philistine sallied forth morning and evening and made his stand for forty days, **shouting out: "Is there not a man in Israel brave enough to fight me? Where is Abner, your commander, and Jonathan, the king's son? Where are the mighty men who trust in the Lord your God?" But Saul would not give permission for anyone to fight Goliath. He waited for a sign from the Lord to know what to do.**

When David told Jesse that he should return to minister to the king, Jesse said to David, his son: "Take for your brothers this bushel of parched corn, these ten loaves of bread, and carry them quickly to your brothers' camp, and bring these ten cheeses to the captain of their army unit, give your brothers my greetings and bring back some token from them so **I will know that they are well.** Now Saul, they and all the Israelites, are in the valley of Elah fighting the Philistines." **David knew that his father was very old and had forgotten that he was serving king Saul. He remained silent.** Early next morning David rose, left the sheep with a keeper, took the provisions as Jesse had instructed him. He arrived at the encampment just when the army were going out to the battle lines shouting out the war cry. Israel and the Philistines drew up to their battle lines – army against army. David left his baggage with the baggage keeper and ran to the army. When he arrived he greeted his brothers. While he was talking to them, the champion, Goliath the Philistine from Gath stepped out from the ranks of the Philistines. He spoke as before and David heard him. All the Israelites – when they saw the man – drew back from his presence because they were very frightened. The Israelites were saying **to each other,** "You see this man who comes up. He comes up to taunt Israel. **No doubt** the king will enrich the man who strikes him down with great riches, will give him his daughter and make his father's house free in Israel **from all levies due to the king."**

David said these words to the men standing with him: "What **did you say** will be done to the man who strikes this Philistine down and removes this disgrace from Israel, for who is this uncircumcised Philistine that he should taunt the armies of the living God?" The men said to him, "It is as we have said, so it shall be done for the man who strikes him down." Eliab, his eldest brother, heard him speaking to the men and was very angry with David: "Why have you come down? With whom have you left our few sheep in the wilderness? I know your arrogance and your impudence, you have only come down to watch the battles." David replied, "What have I done now? It was only a word." But he went away from him and repeated those questions to others. All gave him the same answer.

When they heard the words spoken by David, they repeated them to Saul and he was brought to him. **Saul said to him, "So it was you who was questioning the courage of my men."** David said to him, "Let no man's courage fail him! Your servant will go and take on this Philistine in battle." Saul dismissed David: "You cannot go against this Philistine to fight him. You are only a lad. He has been a warrior since his childhood." David protested, "Your servant was keeping his father's sheep. When a lion or bear came and took a lamb from the flock, I went after him and struck him down and delivered it out of his mouth. When he rose up against me, I grabbed him by his beard and struck him and killed him. Your servant killed both lions and bears and this uncircumcised Philistine shall be as one of them because he has taunted the armies of the living God." David carried on saying, "The LORD who delivered me out of the might of the lion and the bear will deliver me from this Philistine."

Saul listened to David and thought, "This was a sign from the Lord. Only the Lord could deliver Israel from this Philistine and the spirit of the Lord was with David." Saul said to him, "Go then and the LORD be with you." Saul had David dressed in his own clothing. He placed a bronze helmet on him and clothed him with a coat of mail. David girded his sword upon his military gear and tried to move but could not for he was not used to the weight. David said to Saul, "I cannot go out in these for I am not used to them." So David took them off, but instead took his staff in his hand, went and chose five smooth stones from the wadi, put them into the pocket of his shepherd's bag. His sling was in his hand when he approached the Philistine.

The Philistine came closer to David with his shield bearer ahead of him. The Philistine looked and saw David and scorned him because he was but a ruddy, good looking lad. The Philistine mocked him, "Am I a dog that you come to me carrying stones?" The Philistine then cursed David by his gods. The Philistines said to David, "Come closer to me and I will give your flesh to the birds of the skies and to the beasts of the field." David responded to the Philistine, "You approach me with a sword, a javelin and a scimitar but I come to you in the name of the LORD of hosts, the God of the armies of Israel whom you have mocked. Today the LORD will deliver you into my hand and I will strike you down and cut your head off. I will give the corpses of the Philistine camp this very day to the birds and the wild beasts of the earth, that the whole world will know that there is a God in Israel and that all assembled here will know that the LORD does not save by the sword or javelin because the LORD controls all battles. He will deliver you into our hands." When the Philistine proceeded to come closer to David, he ran quickly towards the Philistine ranks to take on the Philistine. David put his hand in his bag, took a stone and slung it and struck the Philistine in his forehead; the stone sank into his forehead and he fell face to the ground.

Thus did David prevail over the Philistine with a sling and stone. He struck down the Philistine and stunned him without a sword in his possession. David ran and stood by the Philistine. He took his sword, drew it out of the sheath and killed him by cutting off his head. When the Philistines saw that their hero was dead, they fled. The forces of Israel and Judah proceeded, shouting, and pursued the Philistines up to the approach to Gai, even to the gates of Ekron. The wounded of the Philistines were strewn all the way to Shaaraim, to Gath and Ekron. The armies of Israel returned from the chase after the Philistines and plundered their encampment. David eventually brought the head to Jerusalem but kept the giant's armour in his tent as a trophy. **Goliath's sword he gave to the priests as an offering to the Lord.**

When Saul saw David go up against the Philistine, **to kill him with a sling and stone, and lift up his sword to cut off his head,** he **trembled and** said to Abner, the commander of his army, "This youth, **David,** whose son is he? **Does he come from a distinguished family?" For Saul could not forget the words of Samuel, "The Lord has torn away the kingdom of Israel from you this day and has granted it to a man worthier than you." Was this David, who comforted him with the music of the lyre, who slew lions and bears and killed giants with a sling, the man chosen by the Lord to take away his kingdom?** Abner answered: "By your life, O king, I do not know." The king ordered him, "You must ask whose son is this stripling."

So when David returned from striking down the Philistine, Abner intercepted him and ushered him to Saul. He was still holding the head of the Philistine. Saul asked him, "Young man, **my David,** whose son are you?" David replied, "Only the son of your subject, Jesse the Bethlehemite." **Saul said, "So you are from Judah. Is your father happy to serve a king from the tribe of Benjamin?"** David bowed and replied, "My lord, you are God's anointed and have saved Israel. My father and my father's house serve you with gladness."

— "Well said, my son, have you ever met Samuel the seer?"
— "Yes, my lord, when he came to Bethlehem to sacrifice. My father and my seven brothers and I joined in the meal."
— "Did he speak to you, my son?"
— "No, my lord, who am I that he should speak to me? He only spoke to the elders of Bethlehem."
— "No more shall you return to your father's home but you will stay with me. You shall continue to play for me and become my officer."

Jonathan's love for David

When David's audience with Saul was finished **and he left his tent, Jonathan went up to him: "You have been chosen by the Lord." He embraced him. From that day on,** the soul of Jonathan bonded with the soul of David; Jonathan loved him as his own life. On that day Saul retained him in his service and did not permit him to return to his father's house. Then Jonathan made a pact with David because he loved him as much as he loved himself. He took off his cloak and gave it to David as well as his coat of armour, even his own sword and his bow and belt.

So David would go out to battle. On whatever mission Saul sent him he was successful. Saul appointed him over his soldiers. This pleased all the people, even Saul's retinue of ministers and servants. So it happened, when David returned from defeating the Philistines, the women from all the towns of Israel would go out singing and dancing joyously with timbrels and triangles to welcome Saul their king. The women merrily sang these words: "Saul has slain his thousands, David his tens of thousands." Saul was very angry because the matter so displeased him. He raged: "David is credited with tens of thousands, I am only credited with thousands. Now, all that is missing for him is the kingdom." From that day on, Saul looked at David with envy and suspicion. **He did not forget Samuel's words: "The Lord has rejected you from being king over Israel.** The very next day an evil spirit from God overwhelmed Saul. He went raving through the house **from room to room.** David was playing the lyre as he did daily **at Saul's bidding.** Saul had his javelin in his hand. Saul hurled the javelin, for he said, "I will pin David to the wall." Twice did David avert Saul's attack.

Saul was afraid of David because the LORD was with him but had departed from Saul **because he believed that** the LORD had rejected him. **Saul could no longer bear David's presence.** So Saul turned him out from his court and appointed him a captain over a company of a thousand soldiers. Thus did David go out to do battle and return to the people. David was successful in whatever he did – the LORD was with him. When Saul saw his great success, he was in awe of him. All the people of Israel and Judah loved David because he went out to battle and returned to them victorious.

Saul said to David, "Here is my eldest daughter, Merab. I will give her to you in marriage, only be you my warrior to fight the LORD's battles." For Saul thought, "Let not my hand be used against him, rather let the might of the Philistines cause his death." But David objected, "Who am I, what status have I, or my father's family in Israel, that I should be the king's son-in-law?" But at the time when Merab, Saul's daughter, should have been given to David, she was given in marriage to Adriel the Meholathite. Michal, Saul's daughter, however, loved David. This was told to Saul and it pleased him for he thought, "I will give her to him. She will be a snare for him so that the Philistines may kill him." Saul said to him, "You can today become my son-in-law through marrying my second daughter." **David did not trust Saul's word.**

Saul then instructed his ministers to speak privately to David saying, "The king is well disposed to you and all his servants like you. Why not become the king's son-in-law?" Saul's ministers spoke these words into David's ears but David rebuffed them: "Do you think it is a simple matter to become the king's son-in-law, when I am a poor man and of no consequence?" Saul's ministers repeated the words spoken by David. Saul said, "Thus shall you speak to David, 'The king has no desire for a dowry, only a hundred Philistine foreskins to be avenged of the king's enemies.'" For Saul schemed to make David fall by the hand of the Philistines. When his servants told this to David, the idea of becoming son in law to the king pleased him. Before the days had expired for meeting this condition, David and his men proceeded to go out and kill two hundred Philistines and David brought their foreskins. They were counted out before the king, and he became the king's son-in-law. **He hid his displeasure from David.** So did Saul give Michal his daughter to him in marriage.

Saul realized then that the LORD was with David and that Michal, his daughter, really loved him. Saul became even more anxious about David and he became his enemy for the rest of his days. Then did the Philistine chiefs go out to war and, whenever they engaged in battle against Israel, David was more victorious than all of Saul's captains so that his name grew in fame.

Saul encouraged Jonathan his son and all his ministers to kill David. But Jonathan took great pleasure in David's friendship. He **told his father, "David does not want your throne, he always speaks with humility. He loves you as he loves me." But Saul**

**became angry, "He is deceiving you with his false words. He will
not rest until he has become the king of Israel and Judah."** So
Jonathan told David, "Saul, my father, is determined to kill you.
Please, take care this morning. Find a secret place and hide yourself. I will go out and stay by my father in the field where you
hide. I will speak to my father about you and tell you what I
learn." Jonathan spoke positively about David to Saul, "Let not
the king sin against his servant, against David, because he has
not sinned against you and because his achievements have given
you great benefit. He has put his life in your hand and has defeated
the Philistines. The LORD has accomplished a great salvation for
all of Israel. You saw it and rejoiced in it. Why should you sin
against innnocent blood, to murder David without cause?" Saul
was persuaded by Jonathan, and Saul swore, "As the LORD lives,
he shall not be put to death." Jonathan beckoned to David and
told him what had occurred. Jonathan brought David to Saul and
he served him as before.

War resumed, so David went out to fight the Philistines and
inflicted upon them a devastating defeat. They fled at the sight
of him. Again an evil mood from the LORD came upon Saul. He
was sitting in his room and was holding a javelin while David
was playing for him. Saul tried to kill David by pinning him
against the wall with his javelin. But he avoided his attack. The
javelin hit the wall. David ran off and escaped that night. Saul
sent soldiers to David's home to keep an eye on him and to kill
him in the morning. Michal, David's wife, warned him, "If you
do not save your life tonight, tomorrow you will be dead." Michal
lowered David through the window. He successfully made his
escape. Michal took the image of her household god and put it
on the bed, a cushion of goats' hair at the top which she covered
with a sheet. When Saul sent his officers to arrest David, she
protested, "He is ill." Saul sent the officers to look for David with
these words, "Bring him to me even from his bed, so that I may

kill him." When the officers forced themselves in, **what did they see but** the household god with its head of a cushion of goats' hair. Saul reprimanded Michal, "Why have you so deceived me; to send off my enemy so that he has successfully escaped?" Michal defended herself **by lying to her father.** "He threatened me with these words, 'Help me escape, why should I kill you!'"

David ran away and escaped to Samuel at Ramah. He told him everything that Saul had tried to do to him. He went with Samuel for refuge to the dwelling of the dervishes. Saul was told, "David is at the dwelling of the dervishes in Ramah." **David said to his ministers, "He has fled to Samuel at Ramah."** So Saul sent soldiers to capture David but, when they saw the company of dervishes chanting and dancing ecstatically with Samuel at their head, a divine spirit came over Saul's soldiers and they also danced ecstatically. When Saul was told this, he sent other soldiers. They too joined the ecstatic chanting and dancing. Saul sent soldiers a third time; they too became ecstatic. **When Saul was told this, he was beside himself with anger. He said, "I will go myself to kill him."** So he came to Ramah and demanded, "Where are Samuel and David?" One person answered him, "They are at the dwelling of the dervishes." So he went to the place in Ramah **with his men to kill him.** The spirit of God took him over. **In a craze**, he moved to and fro ecstatically chanting until he reached the place in Ramah. There he stripped off his clothes and was ecstatic in front of Samuel. He collapsed while naked and slept the whole day and night. Another reason for the proverb: Is Saul also among the dervishes?

David fled from Ramah and came to Jonathan after a number of days in hiding. He said to him, "What have I done? What is my wrong doing? What sin have I committed against you father that he wants to take my life?" But he answered him, **"I know you have done nothing wrong, but my father fears you. Evil moods confuse him. He thinks you wish to be king.** But, far from it, you will not die. **I will speak to him.** See, my father does not do anything, either great or small, which he does not tell me. Now why should my father hide this intention **from me?** It is not so that he really wishes to kill you. I have spoken to him. He confesses that an evil spirit overtook him and that he wishes your return to his house. He swears to do you no harm."

But David swore, "Your father knows how much you like me. Therefore he says, 'Let not Jonathan know lest it make him unhappy,' but as the LORD lives, and by your life, there is but a step between me and death." Jonathan said to David, "Whatever you require of me, I will do." David replied, **"Tell your father that I have returned to him.** Tomorrow, being the festival of the new moon, I should be sitting with the king to eat, but give me permission to go that I might stay away until the third evening when I will hide myself in the nearby field. If your father misses me, then say, 'David asked my permission to hasten to Bethlehem, his city, because it is the occasion of the family's annual sacrifice.' If he says, 'That is well,' your servant will be reassured, but if he becomes angry, then know that his intentions are evil. Please deal kindly with your servant because you joined in a pact of friendship with me in the LORD's name. And if there is any iniquity in me, kill me yourself, for why bring me to your father, **who will kill me?"**

Jonathan protested, "How can you think that if I knew that my father's intentions against you were evil, that I would not tell you?" David then replied, "Who will tell me then if your father replies to you angrily **when you tell him I have gone to Bethlehem?"** Jonathan said to David, "Come, let us go into the field, **where I will tell you my plan."** Both of them moved into the field. Jonathan said unto David, "The LORD, the God of Israel is my witness: when I have sounded out my father about this time tomorrow or on the third day, if the response to you is positive, shall I not send someone to tell you of it? The LORD do to me then what my father proposes to do to you, even more should my father determine to do you evil and I do not tell you to send you safely away. **If this is my father's will, he cannot succeed. He will surrender his kingdom to you as Samuel has prophesied.** If this be so, let the LORD be with you as he was with my father **until now.**

"**And when you become king,** you will not only show me the gracious kindness of the LORD that I not be killed **as a challenger to your throne,** but also that you will not cut off your gracious kindness from my descendants for ever as the LORD has removed his grace from your enemies, each and every one who treads on the face of the earth." So did Jonathan make a covenant with the House of David: "**If I do not fulfil my promise,** may the LORD seek revenge from David's enemies." Jonathan made David swear again **his undertaking to protect his descendants,** by the love he had for him, because he, Jonathan, loved him as much as he loved his own life.

Jonathan **revealed his own plan to David and** said to him, "**As you said,** tomorrow is the festival of the new moon and, **as I have told him you have returned to the court** since your place will be empty your absence will be noted. **I will explore my father's mood.** On the third day after the new moon, you hide yourself carefully; the place to hide **is where we practice archery** during the days of training; stay by the *Ezel* stone. **On the third day** I will **during practice** shoot three arrows to the side to miss the mark. I will send the boy: 'Go find the arrows.' Now if I say thus to the boy, 'The arrows are on this side of you, bring them here,' you are safe and there is nothing **to be concerned about,** by the life of the LORD. But if I say to the boy, 'the arrows are beyond you,' go away because the LORD is sending you away **to save your life.** And regarding the matters of which I and you spoke, the LORD is witness between me and you for ever."

So David hid himself in the field. Jonathan told his father that David had come to him and had pleaded for his life, "I told him that you would do him no harm and I made myself surety for his life." Saul said to Jonathan, "You have done well, my son," but he thought to kill him. Jonathan said, "He has returned to serve you, my father." When the festival of the New Moon was being celebrated, the king sat down in his place as was his custom on the seat by the wall. Jonathan stood up **to show honour to his father**. Abner sat by Saul's side, but David's place was empty. Saul made no reference to it on that day, for he thought, "Something has happened which has made him ritually unclean **and unable to present himself." He hoped this was so for he wanted him back to watch him and to do with him what he liked. "Yes," he thought,** "surely, it is because he is not ritually clean."

When on the day after the New Moon, the second day, David's place was empty, Saul said to Jonathan, "Wherefore has the son of Jesse not come to the meal neither yesterday nor today?" Jonathan answered Saul, "David implored me to give him leave to go to Bethlehem, for he said, 'Let me go, I beg of you, for my family is having a sacrificial feast in the town; my **eldest** brother has said I must come, **for they have not seen me for over a year.** Now, if you care for me, allow me to go to see my brothers.' It is for this reason he has not come to the king's table."

Saul was furious with Jonathan, **for he had determined to kill David on that day.** He shouted at him, "You rebellious son of a bitch! Do you think I do not know that you have chosen David **over your own family** to your own shame, and to cast shame on your mother's **faithfulness, for who could believe that, in protecting my enemy, you are my son!** For as long as the son of Jesse lives on this earth, neither you nor your kingdom will be secure. Now, for this reason, send for him and arrest him for he deserves to die."

Jonathan answered Saul, his father, "Why should he die? What has he done?" **This answer so inflamed the king that** Saul hurled his javelin at him to strike him down. Jonathan then knew that his father was determined to kill David. So Jonathan left his father's table in great anger. He ate nothing on the second day of the New Moon, for he grieved over David for his father had shamed him **by his insane jealousy.** In the morning Jonathan went out to the practising ground at the time agreed with David, and a young lad was with him. He instructed him, "Run ahead and retrieve the arrows I shoot." As the lad was running, he shot an arrow past him. When the lad reached the place where Jonathan's arrow landed, Jonathan shouted at the lad, "Is not the arrow further ahead of you?" **Jonathan emptied his quiver of arrows.** He shouted at the lad **with words intended for David's hearing,** "Be quick about it, hurry, don't hang around!" Jonathan's lad had no idea of what was happening. Only Jonathan and David were aware of the significance of the instructions.

Jonathan gave his weapons to the lad and ordered him to bring them back to the palace grounds. Once the lad was gone, **and David saw that Jonathan remained, he knew that he wished to speak to him.** David got up **from behind the *Ezel* rock** which was by the forest in the south and fell and bowed with his face to the ground three times **to thank Jonathan for saving his life. When he stood up,** they kissed each other and wept alternately but David wept the loudest. Finally, Jonathan said to David, "Go in peace **and take care. If you are the Lord's chosen, you will be king. I will accept whatever the Lord has decided,** for we have sworn in the name of the LORD saying, 'The LORD is witness between me and you and between my descendants and your descendants for ever, **should you be crowned king in my place.'** " He turned away and returned to the city.

David fled to Nob, **which is between Anathoth and Jerusalem,** to Ahimelech, the priest, **the great-grandson of Eli.** Ahimelech came to greet David in great trepidation, **for he knew something was wrong**. He asked, "Why are you alone, without any of your men?" David answered Ahimelech, "The king has ordered me on a secret mission with these words: 'Let no man know of the business upon which I send you and what I have commanded you to do.' So I have sent off my lads to another place. Now what have you here? Can you spare me five loaves of bread or whatever food you have?" **Ahimelech was suspicious for why had he come empty handed with no food or weapons but he was afraid to challenge David.** The priest answered David, "I have no ordinary bread here, but there is sacred bread **intended for offerings of thanksgiving which I could give you** if you have kept away from women **and are ritually clean.**" David replied, "My men and I have kept away from women for three days. When we leave **on any mission** even the men's weapons are ritually clean, even though it is an ordinary expedition, how much more now if the sacred bread **you give me** is to be put in their baggage?" So the priest gave him the ritual bread **used for thanksgiving offerings,** for there was no **other** bread there except the **sacred bread which could be eaten only by the priests,** that was taken by them from the altar of the LORD to be replaced by fresh hot bread as soon as it had been removed. [On that day there happened to be there a man who was one of Saul's household. He was there to meet a ritual obligation. He was Doeg the Edomite, the chief of the herdsmen who served Saul.] David then asked Ahimelech, "By any chance would you have a javelin or a sword because I have not brought with me a sword or any weapons because the king's business required me to leave quickly." The priest responded, "The sword of Goliath the Philistine whom you struck down in the valley of Elah, it is here safely wrapped in cloth behind the Ephod.[1] If you want it, take it, for there is no other sword here

---

[1] The holy vestment of the High Priest.

except that one." David said, "There is no sword like it. Give it to me."

Thus David proceeded to flee that day because of his fear of Saul. He came for refuge to Achish, the king of Gath, **one of the five Philistine city-states.** And the ministers of Achish said to him, "Is not this David, the **real** king of the land? Did they not sing about him as they danced **in celebration of his victories against us,** 'Saul has slain his thousands but David his tens of thousands?'" David considered their words carefully and was very frightened of **what** Achish, the king of Gath, **might do to him.** He altered his appearance before them and pretended to be mad in their presence. He attempted to climb up the doors of the palace gates. He let his saliva dribble onto his beard. Then Achish reprimanded his servants, "When you see a man is crazy, why do you bring him to me? Do I lack madmen **at court** that you need bring me this one to play the mad man in my presence? Shall this fellow enter my house? **Get rid of him.**"

So David left there in a hurry and fled to a cave in Adullam, **which was about twelve miles south of Bethlehem.** When his kinsmen and all his family heard **that Saul sought to kill him,** they went down to him. Everyone that was down and out and everyone who was in debt and everyone who was embittered **with his life** joined him. He became their chief. The men with him finally numbered about four hundred. David went from there to Mizpeh in the land of Moab. He pleaded with the king of Moab, "You know that Saul is seeking my death. **I am afraid of what he might do to my parents because of me.** Please let my father and my mother come and stay with you, until I know what fate God has determined for me." So he left them under the protection of the king of Moab. They stayed with him the whole time that David remained in his stronghold.

But Gad, the prophet, advised David, "Do not remain in your

stronghold but go to the forests of Judah, **for Saul will find you here.**" David proceeded until he came to the forest of Hereth. Saul heard that David's whereabouts were known and also of the men that were with him. **When he heard news of this,** Saul was sitting **to judge the people** under the tamarisk tree in Ramah, with his javelin, **like a sceptre,** in his hand. All his ministers stood by him. And Saul admonished his ministers who stood around him, "Here now, you sons of the tribe of Benjamin, will the sons of Jesse give each of you fields and vineyards? Will he appoint you generals of thousands and captains of hundreds? Why have you all betrayed me – not one of you informed me that my son made a treaty with the son of Jesse, not one of you was sorry on my account to reveal to me that my son conspired with my servant, David, to lie in wait **to destroy me** as he does at this time."

The slaughter of the Priests of Nob

Doeg the Edomite, who was standing with Saul's ministers, answered him, saying, "I saw the son of Jesse come to Nob to Ahimelech, the son of Ahitub. He sought an oracle from the LORD from him. He gave him food and the sword of Goliath the Philistine." The king sent for Ahimelech, the priest and all his father's household – all the priests that resided in Nob. All of them came to the king. Saul said, "Hear now, you son of Ahitub." He replied, "I am here, my lord." Saul admonished him, "Why have you conspired against me, you and the son of Jesse, to give him food and a sword and to ask him an oracle from the LORD, so that he should rise up against me, to lie in wait **for my downfall** as he does now?" Ahimelech answered the king. He said, **"It is not so, I did not know any of this. I thought,** who among all your ministers is as trusted as David. He is also the king's son-in-law who obeys your commands and is held in honour in your court. Have I today begun to ask oracles of God for him? Such an act **of treachery** is unthinkable. Let not the king lay such a thing upon his servant or to any member of my father's household, for I knew nothing about this – **of David's conspiracy against the king** – nothing at all; **this is the whole truth,** no less, no more!"

But the king said, "You must die, Ahimelech, you and all of your father's house." The king ordered his bodyguard that stood by him, "Turn around and slay the priests of the LORD, because they are hand in hand with David; because they knew that he was fleeing and did not tell me." But the king's soldiers would not raise their hands to fall upon the priests of the LORD. The king said to Doeg, "Turn you and fall upon the priests." Doeg the Edomite turned **to draw his sword.** He fell upon the priests. He killed on that day eighty-five men who wore the **sacred** linen vestments. **As for** Nob, the city of the priests, he went there and struck down with the edge of the sword men and women, even children and babies, oxen and donkeys – all by the blade of the sword. One of the sons of Ahimelech, the son of Ahitub whose name was Abiathar fled and told David that Saul had killed the LORD's priests. David said to Abiathar, "I knew on that day, when Doeg the Edomite was there, that he would certainly tell Saul. I have caused the death of all of your father's household. Stay with me and do not be afraid, for he who seeks your life also seeks mine. You will be safe with me."

David was told that the Philistines were raiding the town of Keilah and were robbing **even grain from the** threshing floors. When Abiathar fled to David at Keilah, he came with an ephod **with the Urim and Thummim by which he could enquire of the Lord.**[1] David asked **Abiathar** for an oracle of the LORD: "Shall I go down and fight these Philistines?" The LORD said to David, "Go and

---

[1] This is found in the traditional text at 23:6. I have brought it forward to the beginning of the chapter which is a more appropriate place.

strike down the Philistines and rescue Keilah." But David's men objected for they said, "See, here **among your kinsmen** in Judah we are frightened **of being attacked by Saul's armies,** how much more **dangerous** if we go to Keilah against the armies of the Philistines?" So David enquired of the LORD once more. The LORD answered him, "Arise, go down to Keilah for I will deliver the Philistines into your hands." So David and his men went to Keilah and fought the Philistines. They slaughtered them and were able to lead away all their cattle **as booty.** Thus did David save the folk of Keilah.

Saul heard that David had gone to Keilah. He thought, "God had surrendered him into my hands, for he has enclosed himself in a city with gates and bulwarks." So Saul called all his armies to war, to go down to Keilah to lay siege on David and his band of men. David knew that Saul had devised an evil plan against him. He said to Abiathar, the priest, "Bring the Ephod here." David asked **before the Urim and Thummim,** "O LORD, the God of Israel, your servant has heard that Saul is planning to come down to Keilah, to destroy the city because of me. Will the leaders of Keilah deliver me into his hands? Will Saul come down as your servant has heard? O LORD, the God of Israel, I plead with you, tell your servant." **In response to the last question,** the LORD answered **through the Urim and Thummim:** "Yes, he will come down." When David asked, "Will the leaders of Keilah hand me and my men over to Saul, the LORD answered: "They will."

So David and his men – about six hundred – made their departure from Keilah. They went from place to place, **wherever the land could support them.** Saul was told that David had fled from Keilah, so he did not go there. David camped in strongholds **which he found** in the wilderness. Finally, he camped in the hill country of the wilderness of Ziph. Saul tried to find him each and every day, but God would not deliver him into his power. David knew that Saul was constantly leaving his court to seek to kill him. He remained in the wilderness of Ziph in the forests. Jonathan set out to go to David in the forest to encourage him to have faith in God. He reassured him, "Do not be afraid for my father Saul's might will not destroy you. You will be king over Israel, and I will be your second-in-command. Indeed, my father knows that this will be so." The two of them renewed their pact **of friendship and loyalty** before the LORD. David stayed in the woods and Jonathan returned home.

The Ziphites went up to Saul in Gibeah with these words: "Does not David hide by us in the strongholds in the woods, in the hill of Hachilah in the south of Jeshimon? Now, therefore, O king, come down as it must be your desire to do so. We will surrender him into the king's power." Saul responded, "Blessed are you before the LORD, for you had mercy upon me. Please return and make certain of the place where he is at and who has seen him there, for I am told that he is very devious. Seek out information of all the places in which he hides out and return to me when you are certain **of his whereabouts.** Then I will go with you. If he is there in those parts, I will search him out wherever he may be from among all the clans of Judah." So they departed from Saul to return to Ziph. David and his men were now in the wild steppes of Maon in the Arabah, south of Jeshimon, **some four miles from Ziph.** Saul and his men went out **from Gibeah** to find him. When David was told, he went to the rocky terrain but remained in the steppes of Maon. When Saul heard this, he went in pursuit of him in the steppes of Maon. Finally, Saul was on one side of the mount and David was on the other. David quickly moved to get away from Saul, for he and his men were encircling David and his men and were about to capture them. But a courier came to Saul with the message, "Hurry and return, for the Philistines are raiding the countryside." Saul gave up his pursuit of David and went to engage the Philistines. For that reason, **the near encounter of Saul and David**, the place was called the 'Mount of Conflict'. David went up from that place to make camp in the strongholds near the spring of Gedi.

When Saul had completed his campaign against the Philistines, he was told that David was **hiding out** in the steppes of the spring of Gedi. Saul mustered three thousand of his **best** young men from all of the Israelite tribes to find David and his men upon the rocks where only wild goats pastured. On the way, he passed **caves used as** sheepfolds. Saul went into a cave to relieve himself. Now, David and his men were hiding in the deepest parts of the cave. David's men said to him, "See, the day has come of which the LORD promised you, 'See, I will deliver your enemy in your hand and you will do to him as it pleases you.'" David proceeded secretly to cut off a small corner of Saul's coat. Afterwards, he regretted having cut off part of Saul's coat, **but his men were angry with him for not killing their enemy.** He said unto his men, "God forbid that I should stretch out my hand against my master, for he is the LORD's anointed." So did David restrain his men by his words and prevent them rising up against Saul **to kill him.**

Saul left the cave and returned to the path. Sometime later, David went out of the cave and shouted at Saul **from a distance,** "My lord, the king!" When Saul looked behind him, David prostrated himself with his face to the ground. David said to Saul, "Why do you listen to the words of men who say that David seeks to injure you. Look, this very day, your own eyes have seen that the LORD put your life into my hands in the cave. I was told to kill you, but I had compassion for you and I said, 'I will not stretch out my hand against my master, for he is the LORD's anointed.' Look, my father, see the corner of your coat which is in my hand. I cut off the corner of your coat and I did not kill you. Know then and accept **visual proof** that there is no evil or rebellion in me. I have not sinned against you. Yet you lay in wait to snatch away my life. The LORD judge between me and you. The LORD may take vengeance on my account, but my hand will not touch you. It

is as the ancient proverb states: 'Wickedness only comes out of
the wicked.' **I am not wicked** and therefore my hand will not
touch you. Against whom does the king of Israel campaign?
Whom do you pursue? A dead dog, a flea? Let the LORD be the
judge and exact judgement between me and you, and see **the
truth** and defend me and free me from your power."

When David finished his speech to Saul, he said, "Is this your
voice, my son David?" Saul broke out in sobs and wept. He said
to David, "You are better than me. You have done me good while
I have purposed evil against you. You have explained today how
magnanimous you were to me when the LORD passed me over
into your hand and you did not kill me. If a man comes upon
his enemy, will he safely send him away? Therefore, let the LORD
give you a good reward for how you treated me today. Now I
can but know that you will most certainly rule and that the
kingdom of Israel will be firmly placed in your hand. Swear now
to me by the LORD that you will not cut off my descendants after
me and not wipe out the name of my father's house." David made
this oath to Saul. Saul went back to his house, but David and his
men returned to their stronghold.

Samuel died. All the tribes of Israel joined together to lament his
death. They buried him in Ramah. **David feared that Saul would
be encouraged more than ever to seek to establish the monarchy
of his household now that the prophet who opposed him was
dead. Saul would try to kill David, for Samuel had anointed him
king in his place. So he fled with his men out of his reach.** David
went down as far as the wild steppes of Paran, **south of the
territories of Israel and north of the land of Sinai.**

**In the course of his wanderings, he returned to the strongholds
in the steppes of Maon.** There was a man who lived in the vicinity
of Maon who had **land and** possessions in Carmel **a mile away
from Maon.** The man was very rich. He owned three thousand

sheep, a thousand goats. He was at the time shearing his sheep in Carmel. The name of the man was Nabal and the name of his wife was Abigail. The woman was both clever and beautiful but the man was mean and cruel. He was of the family of Caleb. David heard **from his stronghold** in the steppes that Nabal was shearing his sheep. So David sent ten of his young men with these instructions: "Go up to Carmel until you come to Nabal and give him greetings in my name with these words, 'Hail, peace to you and your household and all that is yours. Now, I hear that your men are shearing. Until now, your shepherds have been **pasturing** with us **in the area under our control.** We never harrassed them nor did any **of their livestock** go missing **because of us. Indeed, we protected them from raiders and rustlers.** Ask your young men and they will confirm this. Therefore show favour to my young men for they come to you on a festive day, **when you are shearing your sheep.** Please give them whatever comes to your hand to your servants, to your son David.'"

When David's young men arrived they spoke to Nabal accordingly in the name of David. As they ceased speaking, Nabal replied to David's servants, "Who is this David? Who is the son of Jesse? Many servants are now breaking away from their masters. **How is he different?** Shall I take of my bread, my drink and the meat I have slaughtered for my shearers and give it to men of whom I know nothing!" So David's young men turned back to the highway and when they returned they told him all that had transpired. David said to his men, "Let every man take his sword." Every man put on his sword. David also put on his sword. Four hundred went up with David and two hundred men stayed behind to guard the camp.

One of the young men, however, informed Abigail, Nabal's wife: "See here, David sent messengers from the steppes to salute our master and he flew upon them in rage. Indeed, the men were very good with us. We were never harassed, nor did we miss anything as long as we were with them when we were in the fields. They were a **protective** wall day and night, all the days we were with them while we tended the sheep. Consider now what you should do because evil is about to come upon our master and upon all his household. **And, as you know,** he is such a brute. No one can talk to him.''

Abigail moved quickly. She took two hundred loaves of bread and two large skins of wine, five muttons, five enormous measures of dried cereal, a hundred clusters of raisins and two hundred fig cakes and she had them loaded on donkeys. She instructed her young men, ''Go before me and I will come after you.'' But she did not tell her husband, Nabal. So it was that as she was riding on her donkey and descending by a concealed road of the hillside, that unawares David and his men were coming down towards her **to reek vengeance against Nabal** – she met them. David was thinking, ''Surely it was for nothing that I guarded all that this fellow had in the steppes so that he lost nothing that belonged to him. And he has repaid good with evil. God do so to the enemies of David and even more, if I spare of all his company by the morning light so much as one person who pisses against the wall.''

As soon as Abigail saw David, she quickly lowered herself from her donkey, prostrated herself before David with her face to the ground. She then fell at his feet and said, ''Upon me, my lord, let be the blame. Only let your servant speak to you and hear the words of your servant. Let not my lord pay any attention to this mean fellow, to Nabal, for he is as his name suggests. 'Meanness' is his name and 'meanness' is his character. But I, your servant, **did not see the** young men whom you, my lord, sent. Now, my lord, by the life of the LORD and by your own life, **by sending me to stop you,** see how the LORD has prevented you from the guilt of shedding blood and saved you from taking vengeance. Now, let your enemies and all who seek to do evil against my lord be like Nabal. Now, this present which your servant has brought, let it be given to the young men who are under the command of my lord. Forgive the impertinence of your servant **in addressing you in this manner,** for **I know that** the LORD will certainly establish your house forever because my master is fighting the LORD's battles and you have never done any wrong. Even though men have raised themselves up to seek your life, yet the life of my master will be preserved by the LORD your God; as for the lives of your enemies, he shall sling them out as stones from the hollow of the sling. When the LORD has fulfilled for my master all the blessings which he has promised you and has appointed you prince over Israel, this, **what you had proposed to do to Nabal but will not do,** will not be an obstacle to your conscience – that you have shed innocent blood or that my lord has taken vengeance for himself. When the LORD has rescued my lord, then remember your servant **for the good counsel she has given you.**"

David said to Abigail, "Praised be the LORD, the God of Israel who sent you today to meet me. And praised be your good sense and blessed be you that has kept me today from the guilt of shedding blood and taking vengeance with my own hand. For indeed, by the LORD's life, the God of Israel, who has held me back from harming you **because of your words.** For if you had not rushed here to meet me, surely there had not been left to Nabal by morning light so much as one person pissing against the wall." So David accepted from her hand what she had brought him. He then said to her, "Go to your home in peace. See, I have listened to you and have accepted your petition."

Abigail returned to Nabal. He was holding a feast in his home – a feast fit for a king. The heart of Nabal was joyous because he was very drunk. She told him nothing, neither less nor more until the morning light. When morning came and Nabal had dried out, his wife told him all that had happened, **how she had prepared a great present for David, how she had met him on the road and**

had prevented him and four hundred men from destroying him
and all his household, not leaving alive any male who pissed
against a wall. His heart died within him and he became as stiff
as a stone. Some ten days later, the LORD struck Nabal so that
he died.

David sends for Abigail

When David heard that Nabal had died, he exclaimed, "Praised
be the LORD who has exacted from Nabal the price of my shame
at his hand; who has restrained his servant from sinning and
who has redressed Nabal's evil doing on his own head." David
sent messengers with instructions to take Abigail as his wife.
When the servants of David came to Abigail in Carmel, they
addressed her with these words: "David has sent us to you to
take you to him to wife." She stood up and bowed with her face
towards the ground and said, "Behold, your servant is ready to
wash the feet of the servants of my lord." Abigail hastened **to do
David's bidding.** She prepared herself. She rode upon a donkey
with her five young women behind her. She followed David's
messengers and became his wife. David had also married Ahinoam of the town of Jezreel. They both were his wives. Now Saul
had given Michal, his daughter, David's wife, to Palti ben Laish
who was from Gallim. **David heard of this but did nothing.**

Again the Ziphites came to Saul in Gibeah to tell him, "Is not
David still holding out in the hills of Hachilah which is by Jeshimon.?" So Saul departed and went down to the steppes of Ziph
with three thousand of the bravest men to pursue David. Saul
pitched his tents in the hills of Hachilah before Jeshimon by the
roadside. David was in the steppes and learnt that Saul had come
after him. He dispatched spies and learnt that Saul had definitely
come. David proceeded to the place where Saul was encamped.
He could see the place where Saul and Abner ben Ner, captain

of his army were resting. Saul was resting within the barricades while the soldiers were stationed around him.

David called to Ahimelech the Hittite and to Abishai ben Zeruiah,[1] Joab's brother, "Who will go down with me to the camp to see Saul?" **Abishai said to David, "It is foolhardy. He seeks to kill you and you will go down to him." But David said, "The Lord is my protector. He will not deliver me into the hands of mine enemies. Besides, he will not expect me, for as you say, who would be so foolish as to seek the man who wishes to kill him and Saul is with three thousand men."** Abishai then said, "I will go down with you **but let not Ahimelech go for three of us may be heard as we descend to the camp."** So David and Abishai came to the army at night **when they were all sleeping.** There was Saul sleeping within the barricade with his javelin struck into the ground near his head. Abner and the soldiers were sleeping around him. Abishai whispered to David, "God has this day delivered your enemy into your hand. Now, therefore, please let me strike him with the javelin – one stroke **at him** on the ground. I will not **need to** strike him a seond time." But David said to Abishai, "Kill him not, for who can strike out against the LORD's anointed and claim his innocence? As the LORD lives, **neither you nor I will lay a finger on him,** the LORD may strike him down or the day of his death may come or he may be swept away in battle, but the LORD forbids me to strike out against the LORD's anointed one. Now, only take the javelin which is by his head and the cruse of water and let us go; **so that the Lord and the people of Israel will know that I had great compassion upon the king who came to kill me."** So, David took the javelin and the cruse of water by Saul's head. They left. No one saw them nor knew that they had been there for no one woke up. All were

---

[1] Zeruiah was David's half-sister, the mother of Joab [who became David's commander-in-chief] Abishai and Asahel.

fast asleep because the LORD had caused a deep sleep to descend upon them.

David went on to the other side and stood on a far off hill top, the distance between them being very great. David cried out these words to **Saul's** armies and particularly to Abner ben Ner, "Will you not answer me, Abner?" Abner replied, "Who is that crying out to the king?" David called out to Abner, "Are you not a brave man, who can be compared to you in all of Israel? Therefore, why did you not properly guard your master, the king, to let a commoner kill the king your lord. What you have done is not worthy. As the LORD lives you deserve to die because you did not guard your master, the LORD's anointed one, and now, **if you wish to see why I reprimand you so,** where is the king's javelin and the cruse of water which was by his head?"

And Saul recognized David's voice, "Is this your voice, my son David?" He replied, "It is my voice, my lord, O king. Why does my lord pursue his servant, for what have I done; what wrongdoing am I accused of? Now I implore you, let my lord the king hear the words of his servant. If it is the LORD who has stirred you up against me, let him accept a guilt offering **from me,** but if it be the sons of man, let them be cursed before the LORD for it is they who have driven me out this day, so that I can no longer be part of the LORD's inheritance, **his people Israel. By driving me away from you and my people, they are in fact** saying, 'Go, serve other gods,' **for how can I worship the Lord in foreign lands? I beg of you,** let not my blood be shed upon the earth away from the LORD's presence. **Consider how beneath your dignity it is,** for the king has come out in pursuit of a single flea, as when one hunts a single partridge in the mountains."

Saul answered him, "I have sinned, return my son David, for I will harm you no more because my life was precious to you today. I have been foolish and I have been greatly mistaken." David said, "Here is the king's javelin, let one of the young men come and take it. Let the LORD reward a man for his righteousness and loyalty, for the LORD today delivered you into my hand and I did not strike the LORD's anointed. As your life was today precious in my eyes **so that I showed you mercy,** so let my life be precious before the LORD and let him deliver me from all kinds of distress." Saul said to David, "Blessed are you, my son David, you will achieve great success and overcome **your enemies."** But David **knew that the heart of king Saul had not changed and** went on his way and Saul returned to his place.

David thought, "One day, I will be swept away by Saul's power. There is nothing better for me to do than to flee into the land of the Philistines. Saul will despair of finding me any longer within the borders of Israel, so I shall escape from his might." Thus David proceeded, he and his six hundred men to go over to Achish ben Maoch, king of Gath. David settled with Achish at Gath, he and his men, every man with his family as well as David with his two wives, Ahinoam of Jezreel and Abigail of Carmel, Nabal's widow. Saul was told that David had fled to Gath, so he pursued him no more.

David was concerned over his safety in the city of Gath. The king favoured him now because he was a rebel. But the moods of kings change. Had he not killed hundreds of Philistines and many of their kinsmen could seek revenge were Achish to withdraw his protection? So David said to Achish, "If I please you, give me a place in one of the country villages where I may settle. For why should your servant dwell with you in the royal city **and impose upon your hospitality?"** On that day Achish handed over to him Ziklag, wherefore unto this very day Ziklag belongs to the kings of Judah. The time that David lived in Philistia was a year and four months.

And David would go out to raid the Geshurites, the Gizrites and the Amalekites[1], for they were the ancient inhabitants of the land as you approach Shur, even up to the borders of Egypt. When David attacked **the peoples of the** land, he never left man or woman alive, but plundered the sheep, the oxen, the donkeys and camels and **all their possessions, even** their clothes. When he returned from the raids, he would come to Achish **to give him a tithe of all his plunder.** Achish would ask, "Whom have you raided today?" David lied, "Against the southern parts of Judah, the southern districts of both the Jerahmeelites and the Kenites." **For this reason** he never left alive man or woman to bring them to Gath for he thought, "They would report us with these words: 'This is what David does and this is the manner of his behaviour all the time he lives in the Philistine countryside.'" Achish believed David and thought, **"By what he has now done to the Judeans,** he has made himself totally abhorrent to his people Israel. So he will be my slave forever, **for he will never again be accepted by his brethren."**

Finally, the time came that the Philistines joined their armies together for war, to do battle against Israel. Achish said to David, "Know for certain that you will go out with me in my army, you and your men." David replied to Achish, **"Because you trust me,** therefore you will see what your servant will achieve." Achish said to him, "In that case, I will make you chief of my bodyguard forever."

Now, Samuel was dead. All Israel had grieved over him and buried him in his own city, Ramah. Saul had, **in obedience to the Lord's commandments,** removed those who divined through ghosts and the spirits of the land, **so Saul had no one of whom to enquire how the battle would end for he could receive no**

---

[1] This is an indication that in spite of the ban of destruction against the Amalekites, Saul did not wipe them all out as previously narrated (see p. 36). David's ruthlessness staggers the imagination but must have been common practice against other nations. It must, however, be utterly condemned.

oracles from the Lord's priests or prophets. The Philistines were mustering themselves together. They came and pitched their tents in Shunem. Saul mustered all the armies of Israel and they camped in Gilboa. When Saul saw the size of the Philistine army, he was afraid. He shook with terror. Saul enquired of the LORD. He did not answer him in a dream, nor by the **new** Urim **which he had ordered to be made since Abiathar had fled with the original to David,** nor through the prophets **he consulted.** Saul then said to his ministers, "Seek for me a woman who can raise ghosts and I will enquire of her **how the battle will go**." They said "There is a woman that divines through ghosts at En-dor."

So Saul disguised himself by putting on ordinary clothes. He and his two men with him proceeded and came to the woman at nightfall. He said, "Please, divine for me through a ghost. Summon whomsoever I shall name to you." But the woman replied, "Surely you know what Saul has done, how he destroyed all those that divine through ghosts and spirits? Why would you therefore lay a snare for my life which would kill me!" Saul reassured her, "As the LORD does live, you will not be punished for doing this **which** I have asked. **The woman noted his regal manner and that of the two men with him and thought that he was the king.** The woman asked, "Whom shall I raise up for you?" He answered, "Raise up Samuel for me." **She did not believe that she could raise the great prophet from Sheol,** but when she saw Samuel, **she was frightened and** cried out with a loud voice and complained to Saul, "Why did you deceive me, for you must be Saul!" The king said to her, "Do not be afraid, **just tell me,** what do you see?" The woman said to Saul, "I saw God coming up out of the earth."
– How does he appear?
– An old man comes up covered in a robe.

Saul knew that it was Samuel and he prostrated himself with his face to the ground.

Samuel said to Saul, "Why have you disturbed me, to have me raised up?" Saul answered, "I am sorely distressed for the Philistines are making war against me. God has left me. He speaks to me no more, neither through prophets nor through dreams. Therefore have I called you that you make known to me what I should do." Samuel exclaimed, "Why do you ask me? The LORD has removed himself from you to become your opponent. The LORD has done **to you** as he said through me **he would.** The LORD has torn the kingdom out of your hands and has given it to your compatriot, David. Only because you were not obedient to the LORD's command, by not executing his wrath against Amalek. Therefore, the LORD has done this to you today. The LORD will hand over the Israelites who are with you into the power of the Philistines. Tomorrow you and your sons will be with me, even if it means delivering the entire Israelite army into the hands of the Philistines.

When he heard this dire prediction, Saul immediately threw his full weight onto the ground. He was terrified by the words of Samuel. He lost all his strength, for he had not eaten a morsel of bread during the whole day or night. The woman approached Saul and she saw his state of confusion. She said to him, "See, your servant obeyed you and I put my life in my hands. I did as you ordered me to do. Now, heed the words of your servant. Let me put bread before you. Eat so that you may gain some strength before you go on your way." He refused saying that he would not eat. But his ministers as well as the woman insisted. Finally he was persuaded by them. He rose from the ground and sat on the bed. The woman had a fatted calf in her yard. She quickly slaughtered and cooked it. She also took flour and kneaded and baked unleavened bread. She brought it before Saul and his ministers and they ate. They then rose and departed that night.

Now the Philistines had mustered all their armies to Aphek and the Israelites had encamped by the fountain in Jezreel. The lords of the Philistines marched with their hundreds and with their thousands of troops. David and his men were marching at the rear with Achish. The princes of the Philistines demanded, "What are these Hebrews doing here?" Achish replied to the princes of the Philistines, "This is David who served Saul the king of Israel and who has been with me for many days, even years and I could not fault him since he fell away **from his masters** until this very day." But the princes of the Philistines were angry with him. They ordered him, "Make the man return, let him go back to the place which you have settled upon him. He will not go down in battle with us, for he could turn into our opponent during battle, for what better way for this fellow to be reconciled to his master than by killing our men? Is this not the same David of whom they sung while they danced these stanzas, 'Saul has killed his thousands and David his tens of thousands?'"

Achish then called David and declared to him, "As the LORD lives, you have been honest, and I was pleased to let you join me in battle, for I have not been able to fault your behaviour from the day you came to me until now; nevertheless, the lords of the Philistines do not approve of you. Therefore, return peacefully so as not to displease the lords of the Philistines." David protested to Achish, "What have I done? What wrong have you found in your servant from the day I presented myself to you until now, that I should not be permitted to fight against the enemies of my lord, the king?" Achish replied, "I know very well that you please me as much as one of God's deputies, but the princes of the Philistines have said, 'He will not go up with us into battle.' So rise up early in the morning with the servants who have come with you, **for they still suspect them of loyalty to king Saul.** As soon as you awake and have sufficient light, depart." So David rose up early, he and his men to return by the morning light to the land of the Philistines. The Philistines then went up to Jezreel.

When David and his men reached Ziklag on the third day **since**

73

their departure, they saw that the Amalekites had attacked Ziklag and burnt it down. They took captive its women and all its inhabitants, young and old. They slew no one, but took them with them and went on their way. When David and his men came to the town, it was still burning and their wives, sons and daughters had been taken captive. David and the men with him wailed and wept until they had no more strength to weep. The two wives of David, Ahinoam the Jezreelite and Abigail, the widow of Nabal, the Carmelite, were also taken captive. David was in a dire situation because his men talked of stoning him, because of their bitter anger – each man for the loss of his sons and daughters. But David strengthened his resolve **by his faith** in the LORD, his God.

David summoned Abiathar the priest, "Bring me the Ephod." He brought the Ephod to David. David enquired of the LORD, "Shall I pursue this troop of raiders? Shall I overtake them?" He answered him, "Pursue; you will overtake them and recover all!" So David and his six hundred men proceeded to the brook of Mesor. From there David continued the chase, he with four hundred men. Two hundred men were left behind there. They were too weak to cross over the brook at Mesor. On the route, they came across an Egyptian **faint with thirst and hunger.** They brought him to David, who ordered that he be given bread and water which he consumed. They also gave him a fig cake and two clusters of raisins. After he had eaten his spirits revived, for he had had no food or water for three days and three nights, David then asked him, "To whom do you belong and from where do you hail?" He spluttered, "I am an Egyptian, a slave to an Amalekite. My master left me behind when I fell ill three days ago. We had previously raided the southern borders of the Cherethites and the Judean countryside and the southern of the territory of Caleb. We also burnt down Ziklag." David asked him, "Will you take me to the raiders' camp?" He replied, "Swear by God that you will not kill me nor hand me over to my master and I will lead you to them."

When he led him down to them, they were scattered all over the camp, eating, drinking and carousing – enjoying the great spoil they had plundered from the land of the Philistines and Judah. David attacked them from the twilight of their arrival until night-fall of the following day. Except for four hundred young men fleeing on camels, not one man escaped alive. David recovered all that the Amalekites had taken and rescued his two wives. Nothing was missing: large or small, sons or daughters, or the plunder **which David and his men had looted from their own raids,** nothing that the Amalekites had taken for themselves. David brought back everything. He had all the other flocks and herds driven before their own cattle. **In gratitude for the recovery of their wives, children and possessions,** his men said, "The spoils belong to David."

David reached the two hundred men who were too weak to follow him whom he had ordered to remain behind by the brook at Besor. They ran out to greet David and the men with him. When David approached them, he greeted them warmly. But the greedy and base fellows who went down with David said, "Because they did not come with us, we will not give them anything of the plunder we recovered, only let them have their wives and chil-dren. Let them take them and go." David objected, "Not so, my brothers, you will not act so. That which the LORD – who has guarded us against evil and delivered the band that came against us into our hands – has given to us will be shared by all. Who will take sides with you, who of all my men will side with you in this matter? For spoils will be divided between those who goes into battle and those who stay in the camp; they will share alike." So this became the custom and law in Israel until this very day.

When David came to Ziklag, he sent portions of the plunder to the elders of Judah, especially to his friends with this message, "See this is a present for you from the plunder of the enemies of the LORD; **he sent presents** to them in Beth-el, Ramoth of the south, Jattir, Aroer, Siphmoth, Eshtemoa, Racal, the cities of the Jerahmeelites, the cities of the Kenites, Hormah, Bor-ashan, Athach, Hebron and to all the places where David, and his men used to stay.

The death of Saul and Jonathan

The Philistines did battle against Israel and the Israelites fled from the Philistines and were slain on Mount Gilboa. The Philistines followed hard after Saul and his sons. They slew Jonathan and Anidab and Malchishua, the sons of Saul. The battle went badly against Saul and the archers had him in their range. He was very distressed because of the archers who were pressing upon him. He said to his armour bearer, "Draw your sword and thrust it through me, lest these uncircumcised come and thrust me through with their spears and make fun of me." His armour-bearer would not do this for he was afraid **of slaying the Lord's anointed.** Saul took his own sword and fell on it. When his armour-bearer saw that Saul had died, he also fell upon his sword and died with him.

So did Saul, his three sons and his armour-bearer and all his champion fighters die together on that day. When the men of Israel who were on the other side of the valley as well as those who were beyond the Jordan saw that the soldiers of Israel had fled and that Saul and his sons were dead, they withdrew from their cities and fled and the Philistines came and settled in them. On the day after the battle, when the Philistines came to strip the slain, they found Saul and his three sons lying on Mount Gilboa. They cut off his head, stripped off his armour and sent them with messengers throughout the Philistines' country to spread the news into the temples of their idols and to all their communities. They placed his armour in the temple of Astarte and spiked his body to the wall at Beth-shan. When the inhabitants of Jabesh-gilead heard what had been done to him, **in gratitude for how he had saved them from Nahash the Ammonite,** their bravest men travelled all night and secretly removed the body of Saul and the bodies of his sons from the walls of Beth-shan. They brought them to Jabesh and burnt them there. They took their bones and buried them under the tamarisk tree in Jabesh and fasted for seven days.

After Saul's death, when David had returned from slaughtering the Amalekites, he had been in Ziklag for two days. On the third day, a man with torn clothes and dust in his hair came from Saul's camp.[1] When he reached David, he fell to the ground and prostrated himself. David asked him, "From where do you come?"
– "Out of the camp of Israel have I escaped."
– "What was the outcome, please tell me."
– "The troops are fled from the battle. Many soldiers have fallen and died. Even Saul and Jonathan his son are dead."
– "How do you know that Saul and Jonathan his son are dead?"
– "I was by chance on Mount Gilboa, and I see Saul leaning upon his javelin, and the chariots and the cavalry are on his heels. When he looked back, he saw me and called to me. I said, 'I am here.' He said to me, 'Who are you?' I replied, 'I am an Amalekite.' He then said, 'Stand, I beg of you, besides me and kill me, for the throes of death are upon me, though my life still drags on.' So I stood by him and killed him, because I was certain that he could not survive after he had fallen from his wound. I took the royal diadem that was on his head and

---

[1] He had been the first to find Saul's body. He takes credit for killing Saul and hopes to win a reward for reporting his death to David and for bringing him Saul's crown.

the bracelet on his arm and have brought them here to my
lord.''

David took hold of his clothes and ripped them as did the men
who were with him. They wailed and wept and did not eat until
evening, over Saul, over Jonathan his son and over the armies
of the LORD – the house of Israel who had fallen by the sword.
Then David demanded of the youth, "Who are you?"
– "The son of an Amalekite alien."
– "How is it then that you were not afraid to stretch out your
  arm to slay the LORD's anointed?"
David summoned one of his young men and ordered him, "Go
and kill him." He struck him dead. David said to him **as he lay
dying on the ground,** "Your blood is upon your head for your
mouth did testify against you for you admitted, 'I have slain the
LORD's anointed.'"

And David lamented over Saul and Jonathan, with this dirge: He
said, "Let the sons of Judah recite it as they learn the art of
archery." It is also recorded in the Book of the Just.[1]

The beauty of Israel upon your high places is slain.
How are the mighty fallen!
Tell it not in Gath.
Do not post it in the streets of Ashkelon,
Lest the daughters of the Philistines be glad,
Lest the daughters of the uncircumcised become triumphant.

You mountains of Gilboa,
Let there be no dew nor rain upon you,
Nor fields of choicest fruits,
For there was the shield of the mighty contemptuously cast aside.
The shield of Saul not anointed with oil –
No different from the shield of any commoner.

---

[1] This book has been lost.

From out of the bloody gore of the slain,
Out of the fat flesh of the mighty,
The bow of Jonathan turned not back
The sword of Saul returned not empty.

Saul and Jonathan
Beloved and delightful while they lived,
In death they were not divided.
Swifter than eagles
Stronger than lions.

O daughters of Israel, weep over Saul
Who clothed you in scarlet and in jewels,
Who put trinkets of gold upon your dresses.

How are the mighty fallen in battle?
Jonathan upon your high places is slain.
I am distraught for you, my brother Jonathan,
You were most gracious to me.
More wonderful was to me your love
Than the love of women.

How are the mighty fallen
The weapons of war have failed
To save these valiant men.

After this, David enquired of the LORD: "Shall I go up to one of the cities of Judah?"
– "Go up."
– "Where shall I go?"
– "Hebron."
David went there with his two wives, Ahinoam the Jezreelite and Abigail the widow of Nabal the Carmelite. David also took up with him his men and their families. They settled in the villages of Hebron. The men of Judah came and anointed David to be king over the house of Judah.

They told David how the men of Jabesh-gilead were the ones who buried Saul. David sent messengers to Jabesh-gilead to say to them, "You are blessed by the LORD because of the act of piety you have shown to Saul your master, by burying him **at such risk to yourselves.** Now, let the LORD extend his grace and loyalty to you. I too will reciprocate kindly because you have acted in this manner. Should you need my aid against the Philistines, **I will come to your assistance as did Saul when Nahash the king of the Ammonites came to attack you.** Now, therefore, be strong and valiant, though your lord is dead. But the House of Judah has anointed me as king over them."

Abner, the commander of Saul's armies took Ishbosheth,[1] Saul's son, and conveyed him to Mahanaim. He declared him king over Gilead, the Ashurites (the tribe of Asher), Jezreel, Ephraim, Benjamin and all the tribes of Israel, excluding Judah. Ish-bosheth, Saul's son, was forty years old when he began to reign over Israel. He reigned for two years, but the house of Judah was subject to David. The time that David reigned as king over the house of Judah in Hebron was seven years and six months.

Abner and the ministers of Ishbosheth left Mahanaim for Gibeon **to do battle.** Joab and the ministers of David also went out to battle. They met by the reservoir of Gibeon. One encamped on one side of the reservoir and the other on the other side. Abner said to Joab, "Let the young men make sport before us." Joab agreed, "Let them do so." They stood up and encountered each other: twelve men from Benjamin and household of Ish-bosheth and twelve of the men of David. Fighting in pairs, each caught the other by the head and thrust his sword into his side, so that they fell down dead together. For that reason the place is called

[1] The literal meaning is 'man of shame'. In I Chronicles 8:33, he is called Ishbaal which means man of baal (the Canaanite god, baal meaning master). Both names denigrate Saul's heir and indicate the author's sympathy for David's monarchy.

Helkath-hazzurim (the place of sharp knives) which is in Gibeon.
The battle became very intense that day. Abner and the men of
Israel were beaten by David's men.

The three sons of Zeruiah were present there: Joab and Abishai
and Asahel. Asahel was light on his feet, as swift as one of the
roes of the field. Asahel ran after Abner. In hot pursuit, he strayed
not to the right or the left as he chased Abner. Abner looked
behind him and asked, "Is it you Asahel?" He answered, "It is
I." Abner begged him, "Turn to your right or left and attack one
of the youths, and take his armour **as a trophy after killing him,
but do not seek to get the best of me.**" But Asahel would not
turn away from following him. Abner again exhorted Asahel,
"Stop following me, why should I strike you down to the ground?
How then will I hold up my head before Joab your brother, **for
killing his younger brother?**" But he refused to turn away. So
Abner with the end of his javelin struck him in the belly so hard
that it went through him. He fell down and died in the very
place he fell. When the others of David's men came to the place
where Asahel fell, they stopped **and ceased their pursuit of Abner's
men.**

Joab and Abishai **were not deterred by Asahel's death but** went
after Abner. The sun was setting when they came to the hill of
Ammah that lies before Giah by the road to the forests of Gibeon.
The men of Benjamin rallied around Abner into one troop and
stood on top of a hill. Abner cried out to Joab, "Shall the sword
devour for ever? Do you not know that it will end in bitter anger
**as it did by the death of your brother which would not have
happened had he not pursued us?** How long before you command
your men to stop pursuing us?" Joab replied, "As God lives, if
you had not spoken, I would have done so until the morning
when the men would have dropped from weariness, unable to
keep up with their fellow soldiers." Joab had the horn blown and
his men halted. They stopped pursuing the Israelites and gave up

fighting them. Abner and his men journeyed that whole night through the Arabah – **the wide valley through which the Jordan flows** – and passed over the Jordan, went through the great gorge and arrived at Mahanaim.

Joab returned from his pursuit of Abner. When he had gathered his officers together, there were nineteen men. Asahel was missed. David's men had killed from the Benjamin and Abner's army three hundred and sixty men. They brought up Asahel and buried him in the grave of his father which was in Bethlehem. Joab and his men travelled throughout the night. The day broke upon them only on their arrival at Hebron.

The wars between the kingdoms of Saul and David were unending. David was gaining in power while the influence of Saul's monarchy continued to weaken. **David established his monarchy in Hebron by marrying many women and having sons and daughters.** These were the sons born to David in Hebron. His first-born was Amnon of Ahinoam the Jezreelitess, his second, Chileab of Abigail, the widow of Nabal the Carmelite; his third, Absalom ben Maacah, daughter of Talmai, the king of Geshur. **[So did he seal his pact of friendship with the Kingdom of Geshur which bordered on the territory of Ishbosheth];** his fourth, Adonijah ben Haggith, his fifth, Shephetiah ben Abital, and his sixth, Ithream of Eglah, **whose only distinction was that she was** David's wife. These were born to David in Hebron.

Because of the wars between the houses of Saul and David, Abner gained influence in the royal family of Saul **because it was he who led the armies into battle.** Now Saul had had a concubine whose name was Rizpah, the daughter of Aiah, **whom Abner took to himself.** Ishbosheth remonstrated with Abner, "Why have you slept with my father's concubine?" Abner was burning with anger over the words of Ishbosheth: "Will you treat me like a mongrel belonging to David, **your enemy?** This and every day, I show kindness unto the house of Saul, your father, to his kinsmen and his friends in not delivering you all into the hands of David. Yet you criticize me today for your **sense of** injury on account of a woman. God, do worse to Abner and even more, if as the LORD has promised David, I do not transfer to him the kingdom of the house of Saul and establish the throne of David over Israel as well as Judah, even from the borders of Dan to Beersheba." He did not reply to Abner, so great was his fear of him.

Straight away, Abner sent emissaries to David with this message: 'To whom belongs the territory of Israel? **Were it not for me Ishbosheth would have no place even to rest his head.** Therefore, make a pact with me and I will use my power for your benefit – to bring over to you all the tribes of Israel.' He sent back this message, "I will make a pact with you, but first I require one thing of you, without which you will not see my face **to discuss the matter** except you first bring Michal, Saul's daughter, when you come to meet me." **Abner agreed and told David to make this demand of Ishbosheth and he would have her delivered.** So David sent emissaries to Ishbosheth's with the message: "Deliver to me my wife Michal, whom I acquired for myself with a hundred Philistine foreskins." **At Abner's insistence,** Ishbosheth sent Abner and took her away from her husband, who was Paltiel ben Laish. He accompanied her, weeping as he went, following her as far as Bahurim. Then Abner said to him, "You must go back now!" **Paltiel embraced Michal, wept and** returned home.

Abner began talking to the elders of Israel, **"Before I made Ishbosheth king over Israel,** you wanted David to be king over you. Now, do it, **and I will support you** for the LORD has designated David, for he said, "By the hand of David, my servant, will I save my people Israel from the might of the Philistines and all her enemies. Abner even spoke so to the Benjamites. Abner was busy speaking to David in Hebron telling him how well the negotiations were going with the tribes of Israel, even Benjamin, **the tribe of**

Saul. Finally, Abner came to David in Hebron. With him were twenty men. David prepared a feast for him and the men who accompanied him. Abner said to David, "I will proceed to gather to my master the king all the elders of the tribes of Israel and they will make a pact with you so that you may rule over all that your heart desires." David saw Abner off with wishes for his success.

That very day, the officers of David and Joab had returned from a military excursion and brought back with them much plunder. Abner was no longer with David in Hebron for he had just sent him away. When Joab and all of his army returned, they told Joab, "Abner came to the king and he sent him away in a friendly manner." Joab remonstrated, "What have you done? Abner comes to you. Why have you sent him away so that he is gone **and cannot be fetched back?** You must know that Abner has come to betray you, to learn all about your intentions and what you are doing." **David replied, "I am king and I will do what pleases me."**

Joab slays Abner

When Joab left David, he sent couriers after Abner. and brought him back from Bor-sirah, but David knew nothing of it. When Abner was brought back to Hebron, Joab took him aside between the outer and inner gates of the city as if to confide in him. But he stabbed him in the belly until he died, for the blood of his brother Asahel. Afterwards, when David learnt of it, he cried out, "I and my kingdom are forever innocent before the LORD from the blood vengeance against Abner. Let the crime fall upon the head of Joab and on all of his father's house. Let there be no lack in Joab's household of men suffering from skin diseases or lepers or men too crippled to do anything but work a spindle or slain in battle or without food." So did Joab and Abishai his brother organize the slaying of Abner because he had killed their brother Asahel in the battle at Gibeon.

David ordered Joab and all the soldiers with him. "Tear your clothes, put on sackcloth and wail over Abner." King David followed the cortege. They buried Abner in Hebron and the king cried aloud and wept at Abner's grave and all the assembly wept. The king said this lament over Abner:

Should Abner have died like a knave!
Your hands were not bound
Nor were your feet in chains,
Yet you were slain with no defence
As a man falls unaware before wicked men,
So was your fall.

On hearing this, all the assembly wept again over him. All his attendants sought to persuade him to eat while it was day. But David swore an oath: "God do so to me and more if I taste bread or anything before sunset." The people took note of his behaviour and it pleased them. All the people knew, even the tribes of all Israel, that it was not the king's decree to kill Abner ben Ner. He said to his ministers, "Know that today a prince and a great man in Israel fell. Today though I am the anointed king, these sons of Zeruiah are too much for me! **I cannot restrain them.** The LORD, **not I,** will have to recompense the evildoer according to the measure of the evil he commits."

When the son of Saul heard that Abner had been killed in Hebron, his hands went limp and all of Israel were confused. Saul's son had two men who were the captains of companies of soldiers. One was called Baanah, the other's name was Rechab, sons of Rimmon the Beerothite of the folk of Benjamin, for Beeroth is still considered as part of Benjamin. [The Beerothites had once fled to Gittaim, a city of Benjamin, for refuge and have been residents there until now.] **Now, as to Saul's other heirs to his throne,**

Jonathan had a son who had become lame. **It happened this way.** He was five years old when the news of Saul's and Jonathan's deaths arrived from Jezreel. Fearing for his life, his nurse lifted him up and fled. As she was running, he fell, **broke his legs** and became lame. His name was Mephibosheth.

The sons of Rimmon the Beerothite, Rechab and Baanah, came during the heat of the day to the court of Ishbosheth when he took his afternoon rest. They came into the inner house as though they were collecting wheat, but they stabbed him in the belly. Rechab and Baanah his brother escaped. **In detail this is how Ishbosheth met his end:** When they came into the house, as he was lying on his bed in the bedroom, they struck and killed him, then cut off his head, took his head and went by way of the Arabah throughout the night. They brought Ishbosheth's head to David in Hebron. They said to the king, "Here is the head of Ishbosheth your enemy who sought your life. The LORD has granted my lord the king vengeance this day against Saul and his heirs."

And David replied to Rechab and Baanah his brother, "As the LORD lives who has redeemed my life from every affliction – when one man told me, 'Behold, Saul is dead,' thinking that he was bringing me good news, I had him seized and killed in Ziklag instead of giving him a reward for his news. How much worse if wicked men kill an innocent man in his own home, even in his own bed, will I not seek his blood from your hands and make you disappear from the earth!" And David gave orders to his young men. They slew them, cut off their hands and feet and hung them up beside the well at Hebron. The head of Ishbosheth they took and buried it in the grave of Abner in Hebron.

The elders of all the tribes of Israel came to David in Hebron and spoke these words, "We are your bone and flesh. In the past when Saul was king over us you used to lead Israel in war. The

LORD said to you, 'You will pasture my people Israel; you shall be the prince over Israel.'" Thus did all the elders of Israel come to the king at Hebron. King David made a pact with them in Hebron before the LORD and they anointed David king over Israel. David was thirty years old when he became king. He reigned for forty years. In Hebron he reigned over Judah for seven years and six months and in Jerusalem he ruled for thirty-three years over Israel and Judah.

The king and his men went out to attack Jerusalem and Jebusites who lived there and in the land around it. They taunted David, "You will not enter here. Even our blind and crippled can turn you back." For they were convinced that David could not enter the stronghold. Nonetheless, David did capture the stronghold of Zion which is the city of David. On that day he declared, **"Before the taking of Jerusalem,** I will reward whoever is the first to strike down the Jebusites by crawling up through the tunnel **through which water comes to the inhabitants of Jerusalem,"** for David thought, **"At night when only a few guards are awake, I will send men to climb through the water gutters to reach the city. They will overcome the guards and open the gates, where we will be waiting to enter to take the Jebusites by surprise,** and 'the lame and the blind' will be captured," – the taunt of the Jebusites – which so angered David. Therefore it is still said of a palace which is impregnable: "The blind and crippled are in the house to guard it. They, the robbers cannot enter the house." **Joab and Abishai and a few men waded and climbed through the water gutter which they entered at the spring of Gihon. When they came into Jerusalem, they softly stole through the street until they reached the gates where the guards lay sleeping. They covered their mouths with one hand while with the other they cut their throats. They pushed the gates open. David and his army soon appeared and went through the garrison and houses and killed every Jebusite able to carry a sword.** So David moved his court to Mount Zion and lived in the fortress and called it the City of David. He had more fortifications built around the city as far as Millo and closer into the city. David's power grew and grew for the LORD, the God of hosts, was with him.

So great had he become, that Hiram, king of Tyre, sent emissaries to David with presents of cedar wood, along with carpenters and masons to build David's palace. David realized that the LORD had established him as king over Israel and that he had made his kingdom great, **not for his sake**, but for the sake of his people Israel. David took more concubines and wives when he was in Jerusalem after he had moved from Hebron; so more sons and daughters were born to David. And these are the names of the sons that were born to him while in Jerusalem: Shammua, Shobab, Nathan and Solomon; Ibhar, Elishua, Nepheg and Japhia; Elishama, Eliada and Eliphelet.

Now before David had conquered Jerusalem from the Jebusites and was still living in Hebron; when the Philistines heard that David was also anointed over Israel, all the Philistines went up to destroy David. **So long as the kingdom of Israel was divided between the houses of David and Saul, they considered David an ally, but now that he was king over all Israel, he was a threat to their power in the land.** David heard **of the mustering of the Philistine forces to attack him in Hebron** and went down to his fortress **at Adullam, which was easier to defend than Hebron, nor did he wish to risk the lives of his household or the inhabitants of Hebron.** The Philistines had encamped throughout the valley of Rephaim. David enquired of the LORD. He asked, "Shall I go up against the Philistines? Will you deliver them into my hands?" The LORD answered David, "Go up, for I will most certainly deliver the Philistines into your hands." David came to **a place which was to be named** Baal-perazim. He defeated them there. He cried, "The LORD has broken my enemies with the severity of breakers in the sea." Therefore, the name of the place was called Baal-perazim (the master of breaking waters). When the Philistines retreated, they left behind them images of their gods. David and his army took them away to their own camp.

The Philistines came up again to do battle and again encamped in the valley of Rephaim. When David enquired of the LORD, he said, "You should not go up to fight them frontally, but encircle them from behind. Attack them by the stand of mulberry trees. And only when you can hear the sound of the rustling of the branches as though they were marching soldiers, then attack **for they will not hear you approaching and you will take them by surprise.** For **only** then will the LORD go out before you to smite the armies of the Philistines.[1] David did as the LORD commanded him and defeated the Philistines **all the way from Geba to Gezer.**

Now the ark of the Lord remained in Kiriath-yearim for many years, for the Philistines said that they would attack Kiriath-yearim if their elders surrendered it to the tribes of Israel. David said, "The Lord has elevated me above my enemies. He has delivered the Philistines into my hands and given me Jerusalem as my stronghold. I will now go with a great and mighty force and bring the ark of the Lord to Jerusalem where it will stay forever." So David again mustered the best warriors of Israel, thirty thousand in number. **When the people of Kiriath-yearim saw David's might, they sent emissaries to him and made a pact to serve him. From then to this very day the city was called Baalei-judah (Possessed by Judah).** So David and the men with him proceeded from Baalei-judah to bring from there the divine ark which bears the Presence, even the Presence of the LORD of Hosts who sits between the Cherubim. They drove the divine ark

[1] The author wishes to give God full credit for David's victory to the point of even planning the strategy. As the High Priest's breastplate with the Urrim and Thummim could only give "yes" and "no" answers, David would have had to put specific proposals to God, in which case he would only be giving David's strategy divine approval.

on a newly-built carriage, taking it out of the house of Abinadab
which was upon a hill. Uzzah and Ahio, the sons of Abinadab,
were leading the new carriage. So it was that they brought out
the ark from the house of Abinadab upon the hill – the divine
ark with Ahio leading the ark.

David and all Israel rejoiced before the LORD with all kinds of
instruments made from the wood of cypress trees, on harps, psal-
teries, timbrels, sistras and cymbals. When they reached the
threshing floor of Nacon, Uzzah thrust forward his hand to take
hold of it, because the oxen had stumbled. The LORD was angry
with Uzzah **because of his lack of reverence.** God struck him down
for his rashness. He died there by the divine ark. David was angry
because the LORD had turned his anger against Uzzah. That place
was called Perez-uzzah (burst out against Uzzah) until this very
day. But David was afraid of the LORD on that day, and he said,
"How can the ark of the LORD come to me, **seeing how angry
the Lord is with whoever touches it!**" So David had no desire to
remove the ark of the LORD to him in the City of David. He had
it shunted aside into the house of Obededom the Gittite, **the Levite
from the city of Gath-rimmon.**[1] The ark of the LORD remained in
the house of Obededom the Gittite for three months and the LORD
caused Obededom and all his household to prosper.

King David was told that the LORD had prospered Obededom and
all that belonged to him because of the LORD's ark. So David
proceeded to carry the ark of the LORD from the house of Obededom accompanied by joyous celebrations into the City of David.
So did it happen: when those who carried the ark of the LORD had
gone six paces **without an accident befalling them,** he sacrificed an
ox and a fatted **calf as an offering of thanksgiving.** David whirled
about, **dancing** with all his might before the LORD. David wore a
linen tunic **such as the priests wore.** So David and all the mighty

[1] The description of Obededom comes from I Chronicles.

men of Israel brought up the ark of the LORD with hurrahs and
the blasting of horns. When the ark of the LORD came into the
City of David, Michal was looking out of her window. She saw
King David, leaping and whirling about before the LORD, and she
despised him intensely. They brought the ark of the LORD and set
it in its place in the tent that David made for it. David sacrificed
burnt and peace offerings before the LORD. When David had completed the sacrifice of burnt and peace offerings he blessed the
people in the name of the LORD. He distributed among all the
people, **not only those who were distinguished** but the entire
multitude of Israel – every man and woman – to each person a
loaf of bread, a measure of wine and a sweet cake. Then every
person returned to their homes **with joy and gladness** in their
hearts.

When David returned to greet the members of his household,
Michal came out to meet David. She taunted him, "How did the
king of Israel win glory for himself today, by displaying himself
before the eyes of maids and slaves as worthless men uncover
themselves **in a drunken stupor.**" David replied to Michal, "Before
the LORD who chose me above your father and above all his house
to ordain me as prince over the LORD's people, over Israel, before
the LORD I will continue to make merry. I will debase myself more
than this – in my own sight and with the maids of whom you
spoke will I gain glory." Now, Michal had no child unto her dying
day, **for David never slept with her again.**

When the king was comfortable in the palace, the LORD having
given him security against all his surrounding enemies, **David
wanted to give thanks to the Lord for his kindnesses.** The king
said to Nathan the prophet, "Look, I live in a palace built of cedar,
but God's ark rests in a place, surrounded only by curtains."
Nathan replied to the king, "Whatever is in your heart, go and
do it for the LORD is with you." But that very same night, the
word of the LORD came to Nathan, "Go and say to my servant,

David, 'Thus says the LORD, will you build a house for me to live
in, I who have not inhabited any house from the time I brought
up the children of Israel from Egypt until now, but have sojourned
in temporary tents and tabernacles. In all the places I have gone
with the whole people of Israel, have I ever uttered one word to
any of the **elders of the** tribes of Israel to whom I entrusted the
care of my people, Israel, demanding: why have you not built me
a house made of cedar! Now, tell my servant, David, so says the
LORD of hosts: 'I took you from the pastures, from looking after
the sheep, to become prince over my people Israel. I have been
with you wherever you went and have cut down your enemies
before you. I made your name as famous as the greatest men on
earth. I have found a land for my people Israel and established
her there. She will now dwell there in security; no longer to be
disturbed, no more will evil people oppress her, as at first they
did. From the day I appointed judges over my people Israel, until
now when I have given you security against all your enemies.'
Furthermore, the LORD tells you that the LORD will establish your
monarchy forever. 'When your allotted days on earth are fulfilled
and you will sleep with your ancestors, I will raise your descendant after you – the issue of your groin – and I will establish his
kingdom. He will build a house dedicated to my name and I will
establish the throne of his kingdom forever. I will be like a father
to him and he will be like my son, in that if he does wrong, I
will chasten him with birches and whiplashes as men **punish
their rebellious children.** But my love will not leave him, as I
removed it from Saul, whom I detached from myself. Your house
and your kingdom will be secure forever and your throne will be
established forever'.'' All these words, the entire vision, did
Nathan relate to David.

**When David heard the words of Nathan the prophet, his soul
was lifted up. He wanted to praise the Lord for his kindness.** King
David went in **to the tent in which the ark of the Lord rested** and

he sat before the LORD. He said,[1] "Who am I, O LORD God; what worthiness did you find in my ancestry, that you have brought me to such high estate. But even this was too little for you, O LORD God. You have promised your servant's house success into the distant future. Can any man deserve such divine favour! What more can David say to you, O LORD God, for you understand your servant, LORD my lord. **I know that it is** for the sake of your promises to Israel and according to your own desires that you performed these great victories to make **me**, your servant, aware **of your greatness.** Therefore you have become great, O LORD God. There is none like you, no God but you. It is as all that we have heard **about your majesty.** Who is like your people, like Israel, a unique nation on earth whom God went down to redeem to be his very own people, to establish his fame and reputation, to do great and awe-inspiring things for yourself and your land. You took her to yourself from Egypt, defeating the gentiles and their gods. You secured your people Israel for yourself to be your own people forever; You O LORD became their God. Now, O LORD God, the promise which you made to your servant and his house, confirm it into eternity! Do as you promised so that your name will be magnified forever, that it will be said: 'The LORD of hosts is God over Israel and the house of David your servant is firmly established before you. Because you are the LORD of hosts, the God of Israel who has told your servant your intention: I will build you a house. Only for this reason, your servant has had the courage to make this prayer. Now, O LORD God, you alone are God. May your promises come true – those good things you told your servant. Now, continue to prosper your servant's house that it may serve you forever. You LORD God have declared it! By your blessing, let your servant's house prosper forever."

[1] The purpose of David's prayer, as is Nathan's vision, is to acknowledge the author's conviction that without God, David could have achieved nothing. It is the LORD God who is the hero who has led David to victory.

After this, **when the Lord's ark was returned to the City of David,**
he defeated the Philistines and made them tributaries. David even
captured Metheg-ammah, **the mother of capitals** from the Philistines. He defeated Moab, **and because the king of Moab had slain
his father and mother in whose hands he had entrusted their
lives, David took harsh vengeance.**[1] He made all the men lie down
on the ground, he had them measured with three ropes of equal
size. Two thirds of the men measured he put to death, the men
measured by one length of rope he kept alive. The Moabites
became David's tributaries and paid taxes to him. David also
defeated Hadadezer ben Rehob, king of Zoba, **the Aramean kingdom near Damascus** on his way to establish his sovereignty over
the lands up to the Euphrates river. David captured from him one
thousand seven hundred horsemen and twenty thousand foot
soldiers. He had all the chariot horses weakened by cutting the
back sinews of their hind legs except those required for a hundred
chariots **which he kept for his own cavalry.** When the Arameans
from Damascus came to assist Hadadezer, king of Zobah, David
killed twenty-two thousand Arameans. He established garrisons
in Aram of Damascus and the Arameans became tributaries to
David and paid taxes **to him.** The LORD gave David success in all
his undertakings. He took the gold armaments worn by the ministers of Hadadezer and brought them to Jerusalem. From Betah
and from Berothai, Hadadezer's cities, King David plundered an
enormous amount of brass.

When Toi, king of Hamath, heard that David had defeated all of
Hadadezer's armies, he sent Joram his son to King David to salute
and congratulate him because he had fought against Hadadezer
and defeated him for Hadadezer and Toi used to war against each
other. Joram brought with him vessels of silver, gold and brass.
These also did King David dedicate to the LORD with the silver and

[1] This is based on a rabbinic tradition.

gold that he had dedicated from all the nations he had conquered: Aram, Moab, the people of Ammon, the Philistines, the Amalekites and the plunder from Hadadezer ben Rehob, king of Zobah. David became famous when he returned from defeating the Aramaeans, killing also eighteen thousand men of Edom in the Valley of Salt, **near Beersheba.** He established garrisons in all of Edom. All the Edomites became David's serfs. The LORD gave success to David in all his campaigns.

David ruled over all Israel. David dealt justly and righteously with all his people. Joab ben Zeruiah was commander of his army, Jehoshaphat ben Ahilud was the controller, Zadok ben Ahitub and Abiathar ben Ahimelech were priests, and Seraiah was the scribe, Benaiah ben Jehoiada was given command over the Cherethites and the Pelethites, David's mercenary bodyguards. David's sons were also ministers of state.

David asked, "Is there any person left from the house of Saul, to whom I may be gracious for the sake of Jonathan?" There was a man named Ziba who used to be a servant in Saul's court. He was summoned to David. The king asked him, "Are you Ziba?" "Your servant is he," he replied. The king asked, "Is there a person still alive from the house of Saul to whom I may show great kindness?" Ziba answered the king, "There is Jonathan's son who is lame." The king asked him, "Where is he?" Ziba answered the king: "He is in the house of Machir ben Amiel in Lo-debar. King David sent for him and fetched him from the house of Machir from Lo-debar. **Mephibosheth was terrified by the king's men. Would he be killed because he was of the house of Saul who sought David's life.** Mephibosheth ben Jonathan ben Saul came to David, and fell on his face prostrating himself. David said: "Mephibosheth." He replied, "I am your servant." David reassured him, "Do not be afraid, for I will be kind to you for the sake of your father Jonathan and will restore to you all the land of Saul your ancestor and you shall be a regular guest at my table."

The king summoned Ziba, Saul's former servant, and ordered him, "All that belonged to Saul and his household I have granted to your master's son. You will till the land for him, you, your sons and your servants. You will bring him the profit that your master may have sustenance **here in Jerusalem,** but Mephibosheth shall always eat at my table." Ziba had fifteen sons and twenty servants. Ziba answered the king, "According to all that the lord my king has commanded so will your servant do." **David said to Ziba, "Deal honestly with your master though he is not with you to watch over you, for remember,** Mephibosheth is my guest at table just as one of the king's sons." Mephibosheth had a young son named Mica. All those that lived in Ziba's house became servants to Mephibosheth. But Mephibosheth lived in Jerusalem. He ate regularly at the king's table. He was lame in both feet.

It was at this time that the king of the people of Ammon died, and Hanun his son ruled in his place. David thought, "I will show kindness to Hanun ben Nahash as his father was kind to me **when he gave refuge to members of my family when they fled from the king of Moab after he killed my mother and father.**"[1] David sent his ministers with words of comfort over his father's death. David's ministers arrived at the territory of the people of Ammon. But the officials of Ammon said to Hanun, their master, "You think David does honour to your father by sending comfort to you? Is it not to explore the city, to spy in order to overthrow it that David sent his ministers to you?" Hanun took David's ministers, cut off one half of their beards, **revealing one side of their face,** and cut their tunics down the middle as far as their bottoms and sent them off. **The ministers sent their servants ahead of them to tell David of their disgrace.** When they told it to David,

---

[1] There is no record of this in the text but, see footnote on p.97.

he sent servants to meet them for the men were deeply humiliated. The king said, "Stay in Jericho until your beards have grown back and then return."

When the Ammonites realised how hateful they had become to David, they sent and hired the Arameans of Beth-rehob and the Arameans of Zobah, twenty thousand foot soldiers and the king of Maacah with his thousand men and the men of Tob who had twelve thousand men. When David heard of this he sent Joab and his mightiest army. The Ammonites came out in battle array at the entrance of the gates to Rabbah. The Arameans of Zobah and Rehob and the men of Tob and Maacah were already in the terrain by the city. **When Joab reached Rabbah, he saw the Arameans below the city.** Joab, seeing that the war was confronting him on two fronts, chose the best of the men of Israel and prepared them for the fight against the Arameans. The rest of the army he put in the charge of Abishai, his brother. He instructed him, "If the Arameans are too strong for me, come to my assistance; if the Ammonites are too strong for you, I will come to help you. Be strong and of good courage for the sake of our people and for the sake of the cities of our God. Now, let the LORD do as it pleases him. **So Joab and Abishai led their armies on both fronts against the Arameans below the city and the Ammonites by the gates of Rabbah.** When Joab and his forces encountered the Arameans in battle, they fled from before him. When the Ammonites perceived that the Arameans had fled, they too retreated before Abishai and entered the city and closed the gates. Joab returned from battle with the Ammonites and returned to Jerusalem.

When the Arameans saw that they had suffered badly by the Israelites, they mustered all their forces together. Hadadezer sent for the Arameans that were beyond the great river Euphrates. They came to Helam. Shobach, the commander of Hadadezer's army led them. David was told this, so he mustered all the armies of Israel, crossed the Jordan and reached Helam. The Arameans prepared for battle against David and fought with him. The Arameans, **once again no match for the Israelites**, fled from the Israelites. David's armies slew seven hundred Aramean charioteers, forty thousand horsemen, and struck down Shobach, the army's commander who was killed there. When all the kings who were vassals to Hadadezer saw that they were thoroughly beaten by the Israelites, they made peace with Israel and became her tributaries. So the Arameans were frightened to give any more assistance to the Ammonites.

David and Bathsheba

At the turn of the year, when kings go out to wage war, David sent Joab and his ministers with him and all Israel's armies. They laid waste the Ammonite countryside and besieged the capital Rabbah. But David remained in Jerusalem. One evening when David left his bed **after an afternoon nap** to walk upon the roof terrace of the palace **to catch the evening breeze**, he saw a woman bathing and the woman was stunningly beautiful. David sent someone to find out who she was. He was told, "Is she not Bathsheba, daughter of Eliam, Uriah the Hittite's wife?" **Now Uriah the Hittite was an officer in David's army. He was one of David's thirty-seven mightiest warriors.**[1] **Together with Joab he was laying siege against Rabbah. Now David thought to himself, "See, I am king over Israel and Judah. The Lord has elevated me to be a king over kings. I am too important to camp on the ground with my soldiers who are laying siege at Rabbah. Everything I have undertaken has been blessed by the Lord. There is no more for me to achieve. I know that it is wrong, but am I not king?" Shall I not have pleasure with Bathsheba after which she can**

---

[1] We are informed of this in 24:39. See appendix.

return to her home. He sent messengers to take her and bring her to him. **David said to Bathsheba:**
- "I saw you bathe this morning from my roof terrace. You are very beautiful and I desired you. Will you lie with the king?"
- "It is not good that my lord the king should do so. Am I not the wife of Uriah, a mighty officer in the king's army, who has rejected his gods and now serves the Lord and my master alone?"
- "As I am his master, so I am yours. If it is the king's command, will you sleep with him?"
- "By obeying the king's command, will I not be sinning against the Lord, who has prospered the ways of my lord, his servant?"
- "You are wise as well as beautiful and your words of protest make me desire you even more. If I command you to give the king pleasure, it will be his sin, not yours. I will answer to the Lord. Now, will you obey the king's command?"
- "I will do as it pleases my lord."

He slept with her and **he loved her. It was one week since her menstruation and** she had washed away her uncleanness when she lay with David. **Thus, when** she returned to her home, **and a month had passed,** the woman **knew that she** was pregnant. She sent a message to David, "I am with child. **If my husband does not return from war to sleep with me, when my belly grows my adultery will be known. I will be stoned and I and my lord's child will be killed." David dispatched a reply, "I will send for Uriah your husband and he will return to his house and our guilt will be hidden."**

Then David sent a message to Joab, "Send me Uriah the Hittite **to give me news of the battles at Rabbah."** Joab dispatched Uriah to David. When Uriah arrived, he asked about Joab, the army and the progress of the war. **After he answered all the king's questions,** he said to Uriah: "Go down to your house and wash your feet. **In the morning when you are rested, you may return** to Joab." Uriah left the king's chambers. After his departure, a present of food and wine was sent after him to his home. **Bathsehba told the king's servant, "Thank my lord the king for his kindness but tell him that my husband has not returned home."** For Uriah slept by the door of the palace with the bodyguard of his lord and did not go home. When they told David in the morning, "Uriah did not go home **but stayed with the bodyguard,"** David sent for him and said to Uriah,

- "Did you not complete a long journey. How is it that you did not go home **last night?"**
- "The ark and Israel and Judah dwell in shelters. My lord Joab and the officers of the lord sleep in tents in the open field, how can I go to my house to eat and drink and to lie with my wife? By your very life I could not do this."
- **"The Lord bless you for your righteousness.** Stay another day and tomorrow I will send you back **for tomorrow I will know what instructions to give to Joab."**

So Uriah remained that day and **did not return until** the following day. David summoned him to eat and drink with him. **They talked about the war against the Ammonites and the captains of the army. David asked after his family, his father's house and his wife. Uriah spoke about his father, but said nothing about Bathsheba his wife. David thought, "Has he been told by one of my servants or bodyguards that I have taken his wife to my bed? Perhaps, it is not his loyalty to the Lord but his fear of hearing from his wife what happened between us."** David made him drunk. **He thought, "When he is full of wine, he will speak the truth or he will return to his house and lie with Bathsheba."** But, **he said nothing and** at nightfall went to sleep on his bed in the servants' quarters and did not go home.

That night, David could not sleep because he did not know what to do. The siege of Rabbah could last for months. Bathsheba's adultery would become known and she would be stoned, if she

did not confess that the child was his, for who would dare to kill her without the king's permission. He would be disgraced in the sight of the people. The army would also feel betrayed. It goes out to fight the king's battles while he stays home and lies with the wife of one of his most valiant officers. The Lord had punished him for his sin. But what could he do now but commit an even greater sin – murder. Oh, if he could but end the siege and bring back his army to Jerusalem. Joab would not agree. How could the king retreat for the sake of a woman's life and his own honour. "You are king," he would say. "Order Uriah's death, and he is a dead man." Why is Uriah so stupid. I ordered him to go home. Instead, he would be more righteous than I, his king. Of course, Uriah must know what I have done. There are no secrets in a king's court. He is seeking to bring me down. No man could be so righteous as not to return to the embraces of so beautiful a woman. I gave him the opportunity to save his wife's honour and his own life but he chose to disobey the king and now he must die. Otherwise the House of David will be weakened and the people of Israel will have none to lead them in battle against her enemies. Perhaps, he is totally innocent. No matter, as so many have died so that I could reach my present estate, so must he.

In the morning, David wrote a letter and sent it with Uriah. What he wrote in the letter was: "Place Uriah in the front line of the fiercest struggle, leave him defenceless from the rear so that he may be struck down and die." When Joab read the letter, he asked whether the king had permitted him to go home. Uriah told him what had happened, how the king had asked him to stay for another day and night and that he had slept in the king's court. Joab understood why David had sent him with his own death warrant. He thought, "It is a pity; he is a good man but a fool and he must die. But David will suffer for his death for the matter cannot help but be known." The next day, when Joab was looking at the city, **to see where the battles were being fought outside the city's gates,** he assigned Uriah to the place where the most valiant men of the enemy were positioned. So it was that, when the men of the city went out to fight with Joab's army, several of the soldiers fell. Of David's officers, Uriah the Hittite was also killed.

Then Joab sent to tell David all matters concerning the war. He charged the messenger: "When you have finished telling everything about the war to the king, he may be angry **because I allowed our men to fight close to the city's walls.** When he asks 'Why did you fight so close to the city. Surely you knew that they would shoot arrows from the ramparts! **What stupidity!** By fighting so close to the walls was not Abimelech ben Jerubbesheth killed at Thebez when a woman threw a millstone upon him from the wall? **Knowing the dangers,** why did you go so close to the wall?' Only then say to him, 'Uriah the Hittite is also dead.'" So the messenger went and came and told David all that Joab had said. The messenger reported: "The men were overcoming us and were able to take us on in the fields. We then set them back even to the entrance of the gate. The archers shot at your soldiers from off the wall. Some of the king's officers are dead. Your officer Uriah the Hittite is also dead." **David knew that Joab had chased the Ammonites to the city walls in order to have Uriah slain, though it cost the lives of more men.** David instructed the messenger, "This is what you will say to Joab, 'Let not the battle discourage you, for the sword takes its toll in one way or another. Make an even fiercer attack against the city to overthrow it. Encourage him by these words.'"

When the wife of Uriah heard that her husband was killed, she mourned for her husband. When the period for mourning had passed, David sent for her and she was brought to his palace. She became his wife and bore him a son. But that which David had done displeased the LORD.

The LORD sent Nathan to David. He came and said to him, "There were two men in one town. One rich and one poor. The rich man had flocks and herds, oh so many! The poor man had nothing save one little ewe lamb which he had bought and raised. It grew up with him and his children. It did eat of his own morsel and drank from his cup and lay in his bosom and was like a daughter to him.

"There came a traveller to the rich man. He was too mean to take from his own flock and herd to cook for the guest who had come to him, but took the poor man's lamb and cooked it for the man who had come to him."

David was furious with that man. He said to Nathan, "As the LORD lives, the man who has done this should die. For the lamb his recompense should be four others, because he did this and because he had no pity."

Nathan said to David, "You are the man! Thus says the LORD, the God of Israel: 'I anointed you to be king over Israel and I saved you from the hand of Saul. I gave you your master's house, and your master's wives into your bosom. I gave you the king-doms of Israel and Judah and, if that were too little, I would have added to this much much more. Why then did you despise the words of the LORD to do what was evil in his sight? You slew Uriah the Hittite by the sword and his wife you have taken to be your wife. You had him slain by the sword of the Ammonites. Now, therefore, the sword will never depart from your house, because you have despised me and have taken the wife of Uriah the Hittite to be your wife.' "

Thus says the LORD, "**Beware of what you have done.** I will stir up evil against you in your own household. I will take away your wives before your very eyes and give them to your kinsman; he will lie with them in the light of day, so that all may know. You acted in secret, but I will do this before Israel openly so that all can see."

David said to Nathan, "I have sinned against the LORD." And Nathan said to David, "The LORD has forgiven your sin **for you have accepted your guilt.** You will not die **for the murder of Uriah,** but because your actions have been a great blasphemy against the LORD, **you will reap the fruit of the evil seeds you have sown.** The son that is born to you will most certainly die." Nathan departed to his own home.

The LORD struck the child that Uriah's wife bore to David and he was very ill. David petitioned God for the child. David fasted and, when he came to his room to sleep, he lay **not on his bed** but on the floor. The officials of his court rose to stand by his side, to raise him up from the floor, but he would not, neither would he eat with them. Seven days later, when the child died, David's ministers were frightened to tell him that the child had died, thinking, "See, while the child was still alive, we spoke to him and he would not listen to us. Now, if we tell him that the child is dead, who knows what evil he will do **to himself!**" But David noticed that his ministers were whispering and he knew that the child had died. David asked his ministers, "Is the child dead?" They replied, "He has died."

David raised himself from the floor, washed, rubbed himself with oil, changed his clothes, went into the tent of the LORD, bowed down and returned to his court. He asked for food and it was placed before him and he ate. His officials asked him, "We do not understand your behaviour. When the child was yet alive, you fasted and wept, but now that the child has died, **and you should be mourning over him,** you have arisen and eaten." He replied, "While the child was alive, I fasted and wept for I thought, 'Who knows, maybe the LORD would be gracious to me to let the child live, but now that he is dead, why should I fast? Can I being him back? I shall go to him. He will not come back to me.'"

David comforted Bathsheba, his wife, went into her chamber, lay with her and she bore a son and called his name Solomon. The LORD loved him. He sent a message through Nathan the prophet that his name should also be Jedidyah (the LORD's beloved) to give honour to the LORD.

While this was happening, Joab fought against Rabbah, the city of the Ammonites, and took the royal city. Joab sent couriers down to David with this declaration: "I have fought against Rabbah. Yes, I have virtually conquered the city of waters. Now, therefore, muster the rest of the army and encamp against the city and conquer it **yourself**, for if I conquer it, it will be credited to me." So David mustered the rest of his army and went to Rabbah. He led the **final** attack against it and conquered it. He took the crown of Malcam, **the god of the Ammonites,** from off the head of his image. Its weight was a talent – pure gold with precious stones. It was set on David's head **as the army hailed him for his great victory**. He carried out of the city a huge amount of spoil. He led out the people who were living there and set them to work with saws, threshing boards and axes made of iron or to brick-making in the kilns. David did this to the inhabitants of all towns belonging to the Ammonites. **Once the Ammonites were enslaved in their new quarters,** David's entire army returned to Jerusalem.

The rape of Tamar

Absalom, the son of David and Maacah, had a beautiful sister whose name was Tamar. Amnon, the son of David **and Ahinoam the Jezreelite**, loved her, **but she took no notice of him for was he not the son of her father!** Amnon was distraught to the point of illness because of his sister Tamar. Because she was a virgin, **she was always in the company of friends and guardians.** Amnon could think of no way **to approach or** to have her. But Amnon had a friend, whose name was Jonadab the son of Shimea [David's brother]. Now Jonadab was a very shrewd man. **He was jealous of Amnon, because he was heir to David's throne, and he, Jonadab, his cousin could only ever be his courtier.** He said to him: "O son of the king, why are you becoming thinner by the day? Tell me." Amnon answered him, "I am desperately in love with Tamar, Absalom's sister." Jonadab advised him, "Go to bed and pretend to be ill. When your father comes to see you, say to him, 'Please, let Tamar my sister come and give me bread and cook the food before me so that I might see it and eat it from her hand, **for I fear that I am being poisoned because I am my father's heir.'"**

- "What will I do if she comes?"
- "You will tell her you love her and sleep with her and make her your wife."
- "But she is my sister. The king will not allow it. He will wish me to marry the daughters of a king to strengthen the security of the kingdom."
- "You are the king's son and his beloved firstborn. Once you have lain with her, the king will agree.
- "But if she refuses?"
- "You will take her and then she will have nowhere else to go but into your bosom."

Amnon took to his bed and pretended to be ill. When the king came to visit him, Amnon said to him, "Please let my sister Tamar come and make me two cakes while I watch, so that I may eat from her hand, **for I fear to take food from another."**

David thought, "His illness has weakened his mind, I will do as he wishes." David sent a message to Tamar, **"Your brother is ill,** please go to Amnon's quarters and prepare him some refreshment, **so that he may become well again."** Tamar went to the house of Amnon, her brother. He was lying down. She took dough and kneaded it and made cakes in his presence and then baked the cakes. She took the pan and put them into his plate. But he refused to eat. **Tamar took the plate and returned to put the cakes back onto the kiln.** Amnon ordered, "Remove all the men from my chambers." So everyone left him.

Amnon said to Tamar, "Bring me the food into my room and I will now eat it from your hand." Tamar took the cakes she had made and brought them to Amnon, into her brother's room. When she had brought them near to him to eat, he held on to her and said, "Come, lie with me my sister." She pleaded with him, "Stop, my brother, do not force me. Such things should not be done in Israel. Do not do this abhorrent thing. **For afterwards,** where will I carry my disgrace; and you will be reckoned as one among the common and vulgar men in Israel. Speak to the king. He will not withhold me from you, **and I will agree to be your wife and then will I lie with you."** But she would not listen to her plea. He overpowered her and raped her.

Then did Amnon hate her with great loathing. The hatred he had for her was even more intense than the love with which he had loved her. Amnon said to her, "Get up and go." She pleaded with him, "**Do not do this.** This wickedness in sending me away is worse than what you have just done to me. **You have taken me forcefully, and now you would throw me out bruised and defiled."** But he would not listen to her **for he was ashamed and did not want to see the victim of his spent lust. When she would not go,** he called the lad that served him and said, "Throw this woman out – away from me, and bolt the door behind her." She was wearing a long sleeved robe which reached her ankles, for the virgin daughters of the king were dressed in such clothing. The servant ejected her from the house and bolted the door behind her. Tamar took earth and put it over her head; she tore the long flowing robe she was wearing; she put her hands on her head and walked away moaning as she went.

News of his sister's moaning reached Absalom. He found her in the street approaching his house. Absalom her brother said to her, "Has Amnon raped you? Hold your peace, my sister; he is your brother and heir to the throne. He will say that you seduced him; that he was too weak to force you. Do not think of it. In time I will take revenge for what he has done to you. I will be king over Israel and I will marry you to a great prince and you will be honoured among the princesses of the land. From now on you will live with me until your disgrace is forgotten." So Tamar remained desolate in the home of Absalom, her brother. When king David heard what had happened he was fierce with anger, but Tamar said nothing and Absalom said nothing and Amnon said nothing. So David remained silent and thought this was part of the Lord's punishment for what he had done to Uriah the Hittite. Absalom never said a word to Amnon, neither good nor bad, but Absalom hated Amnon because he had raped his sister Tamar.

It was after two full years that Absalom decided to have his revenge on his brother Amnon. Jonadab, jealous of his cousins, decided to do evil both to Amnon and Absalom. Absalom listened to the words of Jonadab who advised him what to do; he did not know that, through his advice, Amnon had defiled Tamar, his sister. Absalom had sheep-shearers working for him in Baal-hazor which is on the border of the territory of the tribe of Ephraim. When the time of sheep shearing came, Absalom invited all the king's sons to come to Baal-hazor for a great feast to celebrate the shearing of the sheep, for this was the custom in Israel. Amnon sent no answer.

So Absalom did what Jonadab advised. Absalom went to the king and said, "See, your servant has sheep-shearers who are shearing the sheep in Baal-hazor. Please let the king and his servants go with me your servant to the feast I have prepared." The king replied to Absalom, "No, my son, let us not all go and be such a burden upon your hospitality, for my court is too great for you to entertain." But he pressed him to come. He refused but wished him success. Then said Absalom, **as Jonadab had told him to do,** "If you can not, let my brother, **heir to the throne,** come with us **as your representative to show that I have the king's favour."** The king asked him, "Why should he be sent by me to go with you? **Everyone knows how much you please me."** Absalom pleaded with him, so he sent Amnon and all the king's sons to go with him **to Baal-hazor for the celebration of the sheep-shearing. Amnon was afraid, but he knew that the king had been asked to come. Also, Absalom would not strike him in the presence of all the king's sons, so he obeyed his father, the king.**

On the evening of the feast, Absalom commanded his servants, "Mark you, when Amnon is merry with wine and when I tell you, strike Amnon and kill him. Do not be afraid. **I know that he is the king's firstborn,** but you are only obeying my orders. Be strong and brave." Absalom's servants did to Amnon as Absalom had instructed them. **When the guests saw Amnon stabbed in the belly and lying dead,** all the king's sons jumped up and ran to mount their mules and fled, **for they thought that Absalom wanted to kill them all.** While they were on their way **back to Jerusalem,** news came to David, "Absalom has killed all the king's sons, not one remains!" The king stood up **from his throne,** rent his clothes and pounded the earth. All his ministers who stood by him also tore their clothes. But Jonadab **could not keep silent when he saw David weeping and** he said, "Let not my master think that they killed all the youths, the king's sons. Only Amnon is dead, because from the day he raped Tamar, his sister, Absalom had determined this appointment **with death.** Now, let not the king believe that all the king's sons are dead. Amnon alone is dead."

Absalom also fled **from the wrath of David.** The guard who kept watch **on the citadel** looked and saw many people coming from different directions by the hillsides. Jonadab said to the king, **when the guard gave this report,** "You see, here come the king's sons as your servant said, so it is." As soon as he had finished speaking, the king's sons arrived, they shouted and wept **over what they had seen.** The king and all his ministers also wept so loudly **that all of Jerusalem heard.**

When they had stopped weeping, David called to Jonadab and said to him, "How did you know that only Amnon was killed? Were you not here all the time? You knew that Absalom was going to kill Amnon, my eldest son, and you did not tell me. You like Absalom deserve to die, but you are my brother's son, and while Absalom lives you will live, but no longer in my court. The day I see you again, you will die." Jonadab bowed to the king and fled from his chamber and Jerusalem and never saw the face of the king again.

Absalom fled to **his grandfather,** Talmai ben Ammihud, king of Geshur. David mourned for his son **Amnon** every day. But Absalom **was safe because he** fled to Geshur and lived there for three years. The soul of king David was desolate with longing for Absalom, for he was reconciled and comforted over Amnon, seeing that he was dead, **but Absalom was still alive. David saw the hand of God in all that happened because he killed Uriah the Hittite and took Bathsheba to be his wife.**

Now Joab saw how deep was David's longing for Absalom. **He was sad the whole day. He did not send his armies to war to defeat his enemies and to take plunder.** Joab sent to Tekoa and brought from there a wise woman. He asked of her, "Please pretend to be a mourner and dress in the rags of mourning. Do not rub yourself with oil and act as a woman who has been in mourning over her dead for many days. Then go to the king and speak to him as I tell you. And Joab put his words into her mouth.

The woman came to the king's house and pleaded to speak to

the king. The guard said, "The king is not sitting in judgement today. Go to one of the elders who will judge your cause." The woman said, "I must see King David. Only he can protect me. I am a poor widow much distressed. My kinsmen now want to kill my only living son who is my support in my old age. I will not leave the king's house until he sees me and hears my petition." The guard told the words of the woman to David's ministers. They told David, "A woman has come from Tekoa. She is dressed in widow's rags and will not return until you see her. Shall we send her away?" The king rose from his bed and said, "I will see her for she is a widow and the Lord will reward those who show justice and compassion to widows and orphans.

When the woman of Tekoah came to the king, she fell prostrate with her face to the ground and said,

- "Help me, O king."
- "What is troubling you?"
- "I am not merely a widow. When my husband died, your servant had two sons who fought together in the field. There was no one to mediate between them. One struck the other and killed him. Now the whole family have risen against your servant saying, 'Deliver to us him who killed his brother, so that we may execute him for his brother's life' and so they would also destroy the one remaining heir of my husband. They will quench the fire of my coal which remains, leaving my husband neither a remembrance nor a remnant upon the face of the earth."
- "Go home. I will give instructions concerning your case."
- "Let the guilt be upon me and upon my father's house, O lord my king, and not on the king and his throne, **if he lays aside the rights of the blood-avenger to kill him who has killed a kinsman.**"
- "Whoever says anything to you **about killing your son,** bring him to me and he will not harass you anymore!"

- "Please, please, let the king remember the LORD your God **that he make certain** that the blood-avenger destroy no more, lest they destroy my son."
- "As the LORD lives, if one hair of your son's head falls to the ground, **I will be responsible.**"
- 'Thank you, my lord. May your servant speak on another matter to my lord the king?"
- "Speak on."
- "Wherefore have you devised such action against God's people? The king **has declared** that he is the guilty one in that he does not allow the return of his banished son. All of us must die. We are as water spilt on the ground which cannot be gathered up again. God has regard for the living **over the dead,** so let him, my lord, think out a way so that he who is banished may no longer be an outcast from him."

The king looked angry as he heard the words of the woman from Tekoa. She was frightened and she said, "Have compassion upon me, O king, I did come only to speak to you about your banished son, but when you saw my distress and kept my son alive, I thought of your own sadness at the death of one son and the exile of another. But I did come on this matter **of my son** to my lord, the king, because the people about me frightened me, and your servant thought, 'Let me speak to the king; it may be that the king will heed his servant's petition; the king might agree to save his servant from the man – **the blood-avenger** – who would remove me together with my son from **his people Israel,** who are God's portion.'[1] Your servant also thought, 'Let the words of my lord the king give me security, for as a manifestation of God so is the lord, my king, to understand good and evil. Let the LORD your God be with you."

---

[1] By killing her son, she would have no descendants and therefore no portion in God's people.

The king said to the woman, "Do not conceal from me **the truth concerning what I will ask of you.**" The woman said, "Let my lord the king ask **and I will answer truthfully.**" The king asked, "Do I see the hand of Joab in all that you have said?" The woman replied, "As your soul lives, O lord my king, it is not possible to deny what the lord my king has surmised. Yes, your servant Joab instructed me and he put all these words into the mouth of your servant, to alter the situation **between my lord the king and Absalom, his beloved son,** yes, your servant Joab acted in this manner but my lord is as wise as a messenger from God to understand all the ways of the earth." **King David said to her, "You have deceived your king and deserve to be thrashed but because the hand of Joab is in all this, you will not be punished. Now, go."**

David summoned Joab and the king said to Joab, **"Did you think that you could fool me by putting your words into the mouth of a woman? Still your words were wise.** Therefore, I have granted the request **you have made through the woman of Tekoa.** Go, then, bring back the young Absalom. **Let him live in Jerusalem but he will not see my face until I call him to me."** Joab fell prostrate with his face to the ground.[1] He thanked the king and said, "Today, your servant knows that I have pleased my lord the king in that he has granted his servant's petition." Joab left and proceeded to Geshur and brought Absalom back to Jerusalem. The king gave instructions to his court, "Let him return to his house, but let him not see my face." So Absalom returned to his house but did not enter into the king's presence.

Now, in all the land of Israel there was none more praised for

---

[1] This act of prostration by Joab is totally out of character for the man whom David is not able to punish for killing Abner against his will. Is Joab acting ironically in response to David's majestic agreement to what he himself deeply desires? Is his refusal to see Absalom another attempt to save face before his family and the court for his irrational devotion to the conceited Absalom?

his beauty. From the sole of his foot to the crown of his head, there was not a single blemish. When he cut his hair, which he did at the end of the year because it weighed him down, when he had it cut, the hair of his head weighed two hundred shekels according to the royal scales.[1] To Absalom were born three sons and one daughter, whose name was Tamar, **because of his love for his sister.** She too was a beautiful young woman. Absalom lived in Jerusalem for two years without seeing the king. Absalom summoned Joab **with instructions** to win an audience for him with the king. But he would not go to him **because he did not wish to see the king on his behalf.** He summoned him a second time; he still did not come.

Absalom was very angry. Not only would the king not see him nor would any of the king's household. Even Joab who brought him back from Geshur ignored him. He said to his servants, "See here, part of Joab's farm borders on mine. Barley is growing there. Go set it on fire. **Then he will come to me."** So Absalom's servants put the field on fire. Joab rushed to Absalom's house, and demanded of him, "Why have your servants burnt down my field?" Absalom answered Joab, "I sent a message to you. Come here so that I might send you to the king to **say to him,** 'Why have I returned from Geshur? It would be better for me to still be there. Now, let me be allowed in the king's presence. If I have sinned, let him kill me, **for this is worse than death.'"** Joab went to the king and told him **what Absalom had done to his field and the words he said. David wept.** When he summoned Absalom, he came to the king and bowed with his face touching the ground before the king and the king kissed Absalom.

[1] Between 2 to 4 lbs.

Absalom seduces the people

After this, **when he felt secure in the king's favour,** Absalom ordered for himself a chariot and horses with fifty men to run before him. Absalom would rise up early in the morning and stand by the gates of Jerusalem. When he saw a person who had a dispute which could come before the king for judgement, Absalom asked him, "What town do you come from?" He would reply that your servant was from a town of one tribe or another in Israel. Absalom would then say to him, "Your case is justified and correct, but there is no man deputed by the king to hear you." Absalom went on to say, "If I were appointed judge over the land, every man who had a dispute or a cause could come to me and he would receive justice from me." Whenever any man came close to bow down before him, he would stretch out his right hand, take hold of him and kiss him. In this manner did Absalom behave towards all the Israelites who were coming to the king for judgement. So did Absalom steal away the hearts of the men of Israel.

At the end of four years **after his return from Geshur,** Absalom said to the king, "Allow me to go to Hebron to fulfil my vow which I made to the LORD **to do** in Hebron; for your servant made a vow while I lived in Geshur in Aram: If the LORD will bring me back to Jerusalem, I will serve the LORD **by offering him a sacrifice of thanksgiving in Hebron, the city of my birth.**" The king said to him, "Go in peace." So he proceeded towards Hebron, **the main city of the territory of the tribe of Judah, thinking to make it his stronghold when he fought his father for the kingdoms of Israel and Judah.** Absalom had sent spies throughout all the territories of the tribes of Israel, saying to them, "When you hear the sound of the horn, then you will shout, "Absalom is king in Hebron!" Two hundred men from Jerusalem went with Absalom. They had been invited **by him.** They went in innocence, totally ignorant **of**

Absalom's revolt against the king. Absalom also sent for Ahitophel the Gilonite, a counsellor of David's to come from his city, even from Giloh while he offered his sacrifices. The rebellion grew in strength because more and more people rallied behind Absalom.

A messenger came to David to tell him, "The hearts of the men of Israel are turning to Absalom. **He has declared himself king in Hebron and his forces grow in number from day to day, and no one is opposing him. David took counsel with his advisor, Hushai the Archite, who said to him, "Absalom has won over Hebron, the capital of Judah, which should have been loyal to you. He has sent spies to the tribes of Israel in the north and they are rallying to him because they think your power is spent. If we stay in Jerusalem, we will soon be under siege, and will not be able to pick the place for our battle. Also, the inhabitants of Jerusalem may turn against the king in order to obtain food and win mercy from Absalom and his army."** So David said unto all his ministers who were with him in Jerusalem, "Come, then, let us flee the city. Otherwise none of us will escape from the might of Absalom. Let us depart quickly, lest he soon overtake us and we suffer the worst and he wipes out the city with the sword of war." The king's ministers said to him, "Whatever the king chooses to do, we are your servants **ready to follow.**"

So the king departed from Jerusalem together with his entire household. The king left behind ten concubines to keep watch over the palace. Thus did the king depart and all his forces after him, and they paused at Beth-merhak, **the last citadel in Jerusalem on the way to the Mount of Olives. There he reviewed the size of his troops.** All his soldiers passed by his side: all the Cherethites, and all the Pelethites, **loyal men of his bodyguard** and all the Gittites, the six hundred men **from his original band** that followed him from Gath **to Hebron after Saul and Jonathan were slain by the Philistines.** All these men passed before the king. He said to

Ittai, a Gittite, **who had only recently joined his bodyguard,** "Why are you also going with us? Return and stay with the new king because you are a foreigner, even a refugee from your own land. Seeing that you only joined me but yesterday, should I today expect you to become a wanderer with me, seeing that I go wherever I can? Return and take your family with you. **The Lord bless you for your** kindness and loyalty."

Ittai answered the king, "As the LORD lives and by the king's life, only in the place that my lord the king is, whether for death or for life – that is where your servant will be." David said to Ittai, "Go then, my son, pass over before me." Ittai the Gittite passed over with all his men and all the little ones who were with him. All the village people were weeping, crying aloud as the people of Jerusalem who went with David crossed over the brook; and **especially** as the king crossed over the brook of Kidron – all the people crossed over going in the direction of the Judean wilderness. Zadok, the priest, came too. All the Levites were with him, carrying the ark of the divine covenant. They set down the ark of God. Abiathar, the priest, also went up to David when all the people had finished passing out of the city. The king ordered Zadok, "Return the ark of God to the city. If I please the LORD, he will bring me back and allow me to see him and the place where he rests. But if he says, 'I take no pleasure in you,' here I am, let him do to me as it pleases him," **for the king thought that this was the last punishment that Nathan the prophet had ordained in the name of the Lord: "I will stir up evil against you in your own household. I will take away your wives before your very eyes and give them to your kinsman. He will lie with them in the light of day, so that all may know. . . ."**

The king continued to speak to Zadok, the priest. "Do you understand? Return to the city peaceably with your two sons, your son Ahimaaz and Abiathar's son, Jonathan. I will wait in the plains of the wilderness until word comes from you to tell me what is happening." Zadok and Abiathar returned the divine ark to Jerusalem where they stayed. David climbed up the Mount of Olives, weeping as he climbed. His head was covered and he walked barefooted. Every man with him – they all covered their heads; they went up, weeping as they went. Someone told David, "Ahitophel is among the rebels with Absalom." David muttered, "O LORD, I pray, turn the counsel of Ahitophel into foolishness."

Just as David was reaching the summit where God was worshipped **with sacrifices**, Hushai the Archite, **David's aged counsellor,** was coming to meet him, his coat torn and earth on his head. David said to him, "If you come with me, you will be a burden to me, but if you return to the city and say to Absalom: 'I will be your servant, O king, as I have been the servant of your father in times past, I will now be your servant.' Then you will be able to reverse the counsel of Ahitophel. Also, you will have with you Zadok and Abiathar the priests. Everything you hear at court you will tell Zadok and Abiathar the priests. With them are their sons, Ahimaaz, and Jonathan. Through them you will send me everything you hear." So Hushai, David's friend, went into the city. Absalom was about to reach Jerusalem.

When David had just gone over the top of Mount Olives, Ziba, the bailiff of Mephibosheth – **Jonathan's son whom David had given a place at his court** – was coming to meet him with a couple of saddled donkeys laden with two hundred loaves of bread, a hundred clusters of raisins, a hundred of summer fruits and a flagon of wine. The king asked, "What is this all about?"
– "The donkeys are for the king's household to ride on. The bread and the summer fruits for your men to eat and the wine, so that those who are weary in the wilderness have something to drink."
– "Where is your master's grandson?"
– "He remains in Jerusalem, for he said 'Today will the house of Israel restore me to my grandfather's kingdom.'"

– "See, all that Mephibosheth owns is now yours."
– "I bend my knees in gratitude; let me only have your favour, my lord, O king."

When King David arrived at Bahurim, a man came out of there from the family of Saul whose name was Shimei ben Gera. He came out cursing endlessly. He even threw stones at David and at all of his ministers; and this while the troops and all the mighty warriors were **surrounding him** on his right and left. This is what Shimei said as he cursed. "Get ye gone, get ye gone, a man full of blood and wickedness. The LORD is redressing upon you all the blood of the house of Saul in whose place you have reigned. Now, the LORD has granted the kingdom to Absalom your son. You are suffering evil because you are a man dripping with blood." Abishai said to the king, "Why should this dead dog curse my lord the king? Let me go over and remove his head." But the king refused, "What is it that ties us together, you sons of Zeruiah, let him curse because the LORD has said to him, 'Curse David.' Who then can reprimand him by asking, 'Why have you acted so?'" David said to Abishai and all his ministers, "If my son who came out of my loins seeks my life, why not this Benjaminite **who is the house of Saul!** Leave him be; let him curse for the LORD has so instructed him. Perhaps the LORD will look upon my iniquity. **He will see how I accept my punishment** and render me some good for enduring his curses today." So David and his men continued on their way. Shimai carried on walking on the hillside opposite him, cursing and throwing stones and dust at him. The king and all the people with him arrived exhausted **at the Jordan** and stopped to refresh themselves.

By now Absalom and all his troops, the men of Israel, had reached Jerusalem together with Ahitophel. Then Hushai the Archite, David's friend, approached Absalom. He said to him, "Long live the king, long live the king!" Absalom reprimanded Hushai, "Is this your loyalty to your friend? Why did you not go with your friend?'' Hushai answered Absalom, "No, he whom the LORD and this people and all the men of Israel have chosen, his **servant** will I be and with him will I stay. Also, whom shall I serve? Should it not be his son as I served his father? So will I be in your service." **Absalom said, "So be it, old man, serve me as you served my father."**

Absalom said to Ahitophel, "Give me your advice. What shall we do **now that we are in Jerusalem?"** Ahitophel replied to Absalom, "Go into your father's concubines whom he has left behind to watch over the house. All Israel will then know that you have provoked the **irreconcilable** hatred of your father. Then will all those with you be fortified **by the knowledge of your determination to hold on to your kingdom.**" They spread out a tent for Absalom upon the roof and he had intercourse with his father's concubines so that all Israel could see. **So was the prophecy of Nathan fulfilled.** Now the counsel of Ahitophel which he gave in those days was as valued as if a man had enquired of the word of God – so highly valued was Ahitophal's advice both by David and Absalom.

Then Ahitophel advised Absalom, "Let me now pick out twelve thousand men and I will pursue David this very night. I will reach him when he is tired and weak-handed. **When he sees me** he will panic and all his troops will flee. I will only strike the king down. I will bring back all his troops to you. All will return except the man whom you seek **to kill.** But all the people will **be untouched by the war and** enjoy peace." The advice seemed good to Absalom and all the elders of Israel. **But, before agreeing to it,** Absalom ordered, "Summon Hushai the Archite and let us also hear what he has to say." Hushai came to Absalom who said to him, "This is what Ahitophel has advised. Shall we do as he says? If not, you tell us **what you propose."** Hushai said to Absalom, "The advice that Ahitophel has given on this occasion is not good." Hushai continued, "You well know that your father and his men are champion fighters. They are greatly embittered as a bear robbed of her whelps in the wilds, **for they have had to flee from Jerusalem and the comforts of the court.** Your father is a fighter. He will not be staying with the troops **waiting for your attack. He is too clever.** He will hide in some cavern or other **hidden** place. When they, your troops, make the first attack upon them, a rumour may spread **about the attack** that the troops following Absalom are being slaughtered. Then, even those **of your men** who are valiant, who are lion-hearted, will shrivel with fear, for all Israel knows of your father's reputation as a warrior and that those with him are good fighters **who have won victory after victory in the past. Then, they, and not the army of David, will flee and my lord the king will be left alone and he will be killed.** But my advice is: muster to you all the able-bodied men of Israel from Dan **in the north** to Beersheba **in the south,** as many men as the sand on the beaches, whom you yourself will lead into battle. Then we will come upon him in one of his hideouts, wherever he may be found, and we will descend upon him as dew falls on the ground. **He will be overwhelmed.** Neither he nor any of the men with him will remain alive. If he retreats to the city, all the troops of Israel will bring up ropes to that city and drag it down into the valley so that not even one of its stones will be left, **because the forces of my lord the king will be so great that no city in Israel could withstand them.**

Hushai was sent away. Ahitophel pleaded with Absalom to listen to his words but Absalom and all the elders agreed that the counsel of Hushai the Archite was better than that of Ahitophel for the LORD had decided to overturn the good advice of Ahitophel in order to bring evil upon Absalom. Hushai later told Zadok and Abiathar the priests: "So did Ahitophel advise Absalom and the elders of Israel and thus did I advise. **I do not know what Absalom will do.** Now, therefore, quickly send a message to David, 'Do not camp in the plains of the wilderness, but cross over, lest the king be swallowed up together with all his company." Now Jonathan and Ahimaaz were on alert in Ein-rogel, **an outskirt of Jerusalem near the valley by the brook of Kidron, to receive word from their fathers in Jerusalem.** A woman servant would go and tell them **whatever message she had,** and they would go and transmit it to King David. They could not be seen within the city as **going in and out for this would raise suspicions.** But a servant did see them leave Ein-rogel and told Absalom. Seeing the servant, both of them left quickly and came to the house of a man living in Bahurim. He had a well in his courtyard. They climbed down into it. His wife took a covering and spread it over the well's mouth and threw wheat all over it, so their presence would not be known. When Absalom's servants came to the woman of the house, **after searching the other houses in Bahurim**, they asked, "Where are Ahimaaz and Jonathan?" The woman answered, "They have gone over the water brook." When they looked but could not find them, they returned to Jerusalem.

After they left, they came out of the well and went to tell King David. They said to him, "You must quickly cross the river, for so has Ahitophel advised against you. **This is what Hushai the Archite advised but he does not know whose counsel Absalom will follow.**" David and all his company proceeded to pass over the Jordan river. By morning light, there was not one who had not crossed the Jordan. When Ahitophel saw that his advice was not followed, he saddled his donkey, and set off for home to his own town. He gave instructions to his family and strangled himself. He died and was buried in the burial place of his father.

After several days journey, David reached Mahanaim **where he established his headquarters. After mustering all his troops from Dan to Beersheba,** Absalom crossed over the Jordan, he together with all the armies of Israel. Absalom had given Amasa command over the armies in the place of Joab. (Amasa was the son of a man named Ithra the Israelite, **known as such because he lived**

among the Ishmaelites. He had slept with Abigail [daughter of Nahash], the sister of Zeruiah, Joab's mother. **Amasa, the son of Abigail, was, therefore, Joab and Absalom's cousin.)**[1] The Israelite army and Absalom pitched their tents in the land of Gilead. When David had come to Mahanaim, Shobi ben Nahash of Rabbah of the people of Ammon and Machir ben Ammiel of Lo-Debar and Barzillai the Gileadite of Rogelim brought beds and cooking vessels and wheat, barley, meal, dried corn and beans, lentils, honey, curd and sheep and cheese for David and his company to eat, for they said, "The people must be hungry, weary and thirsty **from their journey in the wilderness."**

And David was encouraged by the inhabitants of Mahanaim. They made him javelins and bows and arrows. Many young men of Israel and Judah heard that David was still alive and went to join his armies to fight Absalom, for they heard how he lay with his father's concubines and it did not please them for such a thing should not be done in Israel. Mahanaim became full of men who wanted to do battle against Absalom and to bring David back to Jerusalem. When David numbered the people that were with him, they were so numerous, that he appointed generals over thousands and captains over hundreds. And David sent the army off **to war against the forces of Absalom;** a third of the army was under the command of Joab, a third under the command of Abishai, Joab's brother, and a third under the command of Ittai, the Hittite. The king said to the army: "I will also go with you." The army almost as one said, "You will not go out to battle for, if we flee from the enemy, they will not care **enough to pursue us,** even if half of us were killed, it would not matter to them. **All they**

---

[1] If Abigail was Zeruiah's sister, she was also David's half-sister. David's father was Jesse, not Nahash. This means that Jesse's wife had previously been married to Nahash to whom she bore the two sisters, Zeruiah and Abigail. The narrator makes it appear as if Amasa's birth was the consequence of a one-night stand, thus besmirching his origins.

desire is your life and, were you killed, the battle would end and Absalom would still be king. **Safe in the city,** you are worth ten thousand of us. So it is far better that you remain in the city to inspire us **to victory.**" The king replied to them, "I will do as it pleases you." So the king stood by the gates as the army departed by their hundreds and by their thousands.

Absalom is killed

The king commanded Joab and Abishai and Ittai, "Go gently with the lad, with Absalom, for my sake." The whole army heard David give this order concerning Absalom. The army went out into the field to encounter **the armies of** Israel. The battle was fought in the forest of the territory of Ephraim. The armies of Israel fell before the forces of David. The slaughter was great on that day – twenty thousand men. The battle spread out across the whole countryside. The forest was responsible for more deaths on that day than the sword, **for the Israelites fell into pits and became entangled with each other in the trees and undergrowth and were easy victims for David's soldiers.**

The soldiers of David came upon Absalom as his army was retreating. Absalom was riding upon his mule when it passed under the branches of a large terebinth. His hair was caught up in the lower branches, and he was left hanging between heaven and earth for his mule went on from under him. A soldier who saw it happen told Joab, "I saw Absalom hanging on the branches of a terebinth."

– "You saw him! Why did you not strike him down to the ground? **Had you done this,** I would have given you ten pieces of silver and armour to encircle your waist."

– "Were I to receive a thousand pieces of silver in my hands, I would not stretch forth my arm against the king's son because with these very ears we heard the king command you and

Abishai and Ittai, 'Be careful for my sake with the lad, with Absalom.' If I had dealt treacherously **against the king's command to receive a reward** – and nothing can remain hidden from the king – you would not have taken my side!"
– "I have no time to waste arguing with you. **It is clear that only I have the courage to do what is best for the king.**"

He took three arrows in his hand, **and went to the terebinth to kill Absalom. He pleaded to be released from the branches. Joab said to him, "The Lord, the God of my master the king has ensnared you by your beautiful crown of hair because you wanted to be king in your father's place. The king asked us to be gentle with you, but I will do what is just. Prepare to die. I will cut down your life with three arrows, one for killing your brother Amnon, one for rebelling against your father the king who loves you more than his own life, and one for causing such a great slaughter in Israel. Were I to show you mercy, would you not return evil for good, as when I interceded on your behalf to bring you back from Geshur and then to restore you to the king's court. You stole the hearts of the people of Israel from your lord, your father the king, you drove him out of Jerusalem, you lay with his concubines and sought to kill the man from whose loins you came. Your father commanded mercy; the Lord, the God of Israel, demands justice. You must die so that the pestilence be cut out of Israel." Absalom cried out, "My father the king will punish you if you let Joab kill me." But the soldiers were afraid of Joab and did not move to stop him.** So Joab thrust the arrows into Absalom's body while he was still alive dangling from the terebinth. Ten young soldiers who ministered to Joab then surrounded Absalom, struck him down and killed him. **As Absalom was dead,** Joab blew the horn and the army stopped pursuing the Israelites for Joab commanded them to cease fighting. They took hold of Absalom and threw him into a large pit in the forest, covered him with a great mound of stones and all the soldiers of the

Israelite army fled to their tents. But Absalom had previously built a pillar **to honour himself** in the king's valley, for he thought, "I have no son **worthy enough** to perpetuate my memory." He named the pillar after himself. It is called Absalom's monument to this very day.[1]

Ahimaaz ben Zadok, the priest, said, "Let me run and tell the king the good news of how the LORD has judged **him favourably and delivered** him out of the hands of his enemies." Joab said, "No, do not be the bearer of news today. You will bear good news on another day. This day you should not deliver the news. **He will not thank you for it** because the king's son is dead." Joab instructed the Cushite **who attended him**, "Go tell the king what you have seen." The Cushite bowed to Joab and ran **to Mahanaim to tell the king of the great victory.** But Ahimaaz ben Zadok persisted with Joab, "Whatever the outcome, let me run along with the Cushite." Joab replied, "Why do you want to run ahead, my son, since you will have no thanks for the news you bring?" He rejoined, "Whatever – I will go." Joab nodded assent, "Run then." Ahimaaz ran by the way of the plain **of the Jordan valley – a longer route but easier for running than over the hills, the route taken by the Cushite** – and he overtook the Cushite.

David used to sit between the inner and outer gates **of the city to wait for news of the battle.** The watchman went up to the roof of the gatehouse and on to the city wall. When he looked, he saw a man running alone. The watchman called out and told the king, who said, "If he is alone, he is bringing news, for if he was fleeing from the battle, there would be others behind him." He was coming closer. The watchman saw another man running.

[1] Apparently, the author was aware of this pillar close to Jerusalem which he had to explain away because of his burial in the forest of Ephraim. My intervention is a gloss to account for the information that Absalom had three sons and a daughter.

He called out to the gatekeeper, "See, another man is running on his own."

David: "He too is bringing news."

Watchman: "From the way the first is running, he appears to be Ahimaaz.

David: "He is a good man and must be coming with good news."

Ahimaaz cried out to the king **before he paused for breath.** "Peace." He bowed down to the king with his face to the ground.

Ahimaaz: "Praised be the LORD your God who has delivered up the men who have turned their hands against my lord the king."

David: "Is it well with the young man Absalom?"

Ahimaaz: "When Joab sent the king's servant (the Cushite) and me, your servant, I saw a great commotion and I did not know what was happening."

David: "Stand to the side." The Cushite arrived.

The Cushite: "News for my lord the king. The LORD has judged you favourably and delivered you today from all those who rose up against you."

David: "Is it well with the young man Absalom?"

The Cushite: "As that young man is, so be all the enemies of my lord, the king and all those who rise up against you."

The king was distraught and went up to the room in the gate-house weeping. As he went, this is what he said, "My son Absalom, my son, my son Absalom. If only I could have died instead of you, Absalom, my son, my son." Joab was told, "See, the king weeps and mourns over Absalom." Salvation on that day was turned into mourning for the entire army for they heard that the king was grieving for his son. The soldiers stole into the city that day **quietly and without the shouts of victory** as soldiers steal away when they are ashamed as they flee from battle. The king covered his face and he cried out with a thunderous voice, "My son Absalom, Absalom, my son, my son." Joab came into the king's house and said, "You have caused despair to all your loyal subjects who on this day saved your life and the lives of your sons and your daughters and your wives and your concubines – in that you love your enemies and hate those who love you. For your behaviour today tells them that you give no thought to your officers and soldiers, for I know now, had Absalom been alive and all of us dead this day, you would have been well pleased. Now, get up, go and win over the hearts of your subjects, because I swear by the LORD if, you do not go to them, not one man will remain with you tonight and this will be an evil far greater than any evil that has ever befallen you from your youth until now." The king stood up and went and sat by the gate. All the people were told, "See the king sits by the gate **to welcome the people.**" So the whole army presented themselves to the king. **He praised them for their valour and offered them all presents when he returned to Jerusalem.**

But the Israelites **who had fought for Absalom** fled every one of them to their homes. The rebellious people were divided among all the tribes of Israel. They quarrelled so: "Did not the king save us from our enemies and deliver us out of the hands of the Philistines, and now he needs to flee out of the country because of Absalom! And Absalom whom we have anointed king over us is killed in battle. Now why are you so silent about bringing the king back **to sit on his throne?**" King David sent word to Zadok and Abiathar the priests, "Talk to the elders of Judah. Ask: 'Why are you the last to bring the king back to his house (for petitions had come from all the tribes of Israel to bring him back to his palace **and to reign over them as their king**). You are my kinsmen, you are my bone and flesh. Why are you the last to ask for the return of the king?' And also say to Amasa **my nephew whom Absalom appointed to be his general,** 'Are you not my bone and my flesh? God do to me evil and worse if you do not become permanent commander of the army before me in the place of

Joab.'" **When Amasa received this message from the king,** he
persuaded all the men of Judah. They were as one man as they
sent word to the king, "Return, you and all your ministers."

**When Joab heard the words of the king, he kept silent. He knew
that the king was angry because he had killed Absalom and had
reprimanded him for mourning over his victory. He understood
the mind of the king – to unite Judah and the tribes of Israel
behind him. He would forgive all his enemies so that they would
love him even more. He could despise his loyal officers because
they would not leave him. Joab would wait; his time would come
again. Amasa would die just as Abner had before him for no one
could withstand his might.**

The king returned **from Mahanaim** and reached the Jordan river.
Elders of the tribe of Judah came to Gilgal to go from there to
meet the king, to bring him over the Jordan. Shimei ben Gerar,
the Benjaminite who was from Bahurim, **who cursed the king
after he left Jerusalem,** made haste to join the elders of Judah to
welcome King David. He came together with a thousand men
from the tribe of Benjamin. Ziba, the bailiff of the house of Saul,
his fifteen sons and twenty servants also accompanied him. They
rushed into the river before the king. The ferry boat kept crossing
back and forth to bring over the king's household and to do what
was required. Shimei ben Gerar fell down before the king before
he went to cross the Jordan. He implored him, "Let not my lord
think to punish my wrongdoings, do not remember your servant's
wickedness on the day my lord the king departed from Jerusalem;
let not the king take it to heart. Your servant knows that he has
sinned. Therefore I am the first to come from the house of Joseph
to greet my lord the king." Abishai answered, "Because of what
he did, shall not Shimei die for cursing the LORD's anointed!"
David rebuffed him, "What is it that ties us together that you
should cross me today **by advising me so badly.** Shall any man
in Israel be killed today for do I not know that **once again** I am

king over Israel **and shall I not show kindness and mercy to all
my subjects? If I have forgiven all those who rebelled against me
and sought my life shall I not forgive him who only cursed me?"**
The king said to Shimei: "You will not die." The king swore this
to him.

Mephibosheth, the grandson of Saul, came down to greet the
king. He had neither pared his toenails, nor trimmed his beard,
nor washed his clothes **as a sign of mourning** from the day the
king departed from Jerusalem until he returned home in peace.
(When he had come to Jerusalem to greet the king, he said to
him, "Why did you not go with me **when I left Jerusalem,** Mephibosheth?" He replied, "My lord, O king, my bailiff deceived me;
because your servant said, 'I will saddle me a donkey on which
I might ride and go to the king because your servant is lame.' I
**gave these instructions to Ziba, but he left me behind and took
all the donkeys laden with food to my lord the king.** He has
slandered your servant to my lord the king, for my lord the king
is like the reflection of God. **You believed him and gave him all
that you had given to me. But no matter.** Were not all of my
fathers as dead men before my lord the king **if he had so desired,**
but you did place your servant among those who ate at your
own table . What future claim do I have **to make upon you?** Why
should I cry out any more **protests** to the king?" **The king saw
that Ziba might have deceived him but could not be certain.** The
king **was angry and** said to him, "Why will you go on speaking?
I cannot know who speaks the truth; you or Ziba. I declare: you
and Ziba divide the land." Mephibosheth replied, "Let him take
it all, so long as my lord the king has come back safely to his
own home.")[1]

Barzillai the Gileadite came down from Rogelim. He had escorted

---

[1] This story is out of sequence in order to complete the story of the rivalry
between Mephibosheth and his conniving bailiff.

the king to the Jordan to see him across the river. Barzillai was very old – in his eighties. He had provided the king with food and drink while he dwelt in Mahanaim because he was a very rich man. The king said to Barzillai, "Come across with me and I will **now reciprocate and** look after you as well as myself in Jerusalem," **for he wanted to show his gratitude to the old man.** But Barzillai said to the king, "How many days or years of my life are there left to me that I should go up with the king to Jerusalem? I am now eighty years. I can hardly judge between one thing and another. Can your servant taste what I eat or what I drink? Can I hear anymore the voice of male and female singers? Why should I then be a burden upon my lord the king, **when I will not be able to enjoy the luxuries of the court?** Let your servant just cross over the Jordan with the king, for why should he reward me with such a reward **as to be a guest in his palace?** Let your servant, I implore you, turn back that I may die in my city by the grave of my father and mother. But see, here is your servant Chimham, my son, let him cross over with my lord the king and do for him what pleases you." He replied, "Chimham will go over with me and I will do for him as it pleases *you* and whatever else you would ask of me, I will do for you." And all of the king's household and forces crossed the Jordan. The king crossed over and kissed Barzillai and blessed him and he returned to his own home.

When the king crossed over **the Jordan** he came to Gilgal and Chimham went with him. All the elders of Judah escorted the king and half of the elders of the other tribes of Israel. Then, all the elders came to the king and said to him, "Why have our brothers stolen a march **on us and had the privilege** to escort the king and his household over the Jordan together with all his soldiers?" But all the men of Judah answered the men of Israel, "Because the king is close to us – **he is our kinsman from the tribe of Judah** – what right do you have then to be angry over this matter, **that we were the first to return him to his kingdom?** Have we enjoyed any hospitality, have any gifts been given to us **because of this tribute we pay to our king?"** But the men of Israel retorted to the men of Judah, "We have ten parts in the king **because we are ten tribes, while you are only one,** and we have also more right to **bring back** David than you. **For we were the first to send messengers to the king to come and reign over us again while he had to send messengers to you to ask why you delayed in hailing him as king. And is not Hebron, where Absalom declared himself king, the capital of Judah. You did not oppose him.** Why did you then belittle us as we were the first to move to bring back our king?" But the arguments of the men of Judah were more heated than the arguments of the men of Israel, **because they knew in their hearts that they were wrong. But king David kept silent for it pleased him that all Israel and Judah were seeking to be those who returned him to his kingdom in Jerusalem. But the men of Israel were angry with king David for he had slighted them.**

There was a schemer named Sheba ben Bichri, a Benjaminite. **He saw that the Israelites were angry against David** so he had horns blown through Israel with the declaration: "We have no portion in David neither have we any common ancestry with the son of Jesse. Every man to his own tents, O Israel." **The call of Bichri was conveyed** to the Israelites and they no longer followed David but gave their allegiance to Sheba ben Bichri; but the men of Judah all were loyal to their king **in all the territories** from the Jordan to Jerusalem.

David arrived at his palace in Jerusalem. Immediately, he placed the ten concubines whom he had left to watch over the palace in a separate suite of rooms. He provided them with food **and clothing** but did not lie with them. They were secluded until the day of their death, widows of a living husband, **because Absalom** had lain with them and because they could not marry any other man having been the king's concubines.

The king said to Amasa, **whom he had appointed commander of the army instead of Joab,** "Muster the men of Judah before me within three days – you be here!" So Amasa went to muster the men of Judah but he delayed beyond the time given him. David said to Abishai: "Because of this delay, Sheba ben Bichri can inflict more damage upon us than Absalom. Take your lord's personal militia and pursue him before he captures fortified cities and escapes out of our reach." Following his lead out of Jerusalem were Joab's contingent, the Cherethites, the Pelethites and all the veteran soldiers. They left Jerusalem to track down Sheba ben Bichri. **David did not ask Joab to lead the pursuit because he did not want him to resume command of his armies.**

When they had reached the great rock which is in Gibeon, Amasa, **with the troops he had mustered,** came to meet them. Joab was dressed for battle with a belt around his waist holding a sword in its sheath. **Joab had allowed the belt to hang very** low, so that when he walked it would fall out. **It slipped out when he went to greet Amasa. He picked it up but, in his feigned haste to welcome Amasa, kept it in his hand and did not return it to its sheath.** Joab said to Amasa, "Is it well with you, my brother?" Joab took Amasa by the beard with his right hand as if to kiss him. And Amasa, paying no attention to the sword which was in Joab's **left** hand, was stabbed in the belly **with such force** that his guts poured out on to the ground. Joab did not need to strike him again. He died. **The men with Amasa trembled and did not know what to do.**

Joab cried out to them, "Was this not Amasa the commander whom Absalom appointed to kill David and his soldiers! Was this not Amasa whose rebellion made thousands of mothers and widows grieve over the deaths of their sons and husbands! King

David would have saved Absalom from death. He had mercy on Amasa and made him his commander when I slew Absalom. Now I have slain Amasa, for as Absalom was a traitor, so was Amasa. Both deserved to die. And now, I and my men will pursue Sheba son of Bichri who is also a traitor to the Lord's anointed. Follow me and bring an end to all treachery against the kingdom of David." So Joab and Abishai his brother **and their men** went to find Sheba the son of Bichri.

One of Joab's attendants stood by Amasa's body and said **to Amasa's men as they marched forward:** "He that is for Joab and he that is for David, let them follow Joab **to run to ground Sheba son of Bichri who would be king in David's place."** But, when Joab's men saw that all the soldiers stopped short, as soon as they saw Amasa wallowing in his blood in the middle of the highway, they carried Amasa off the highway onto the field and covered him with a cloak. When he was removed from the highway **so that none could see him** all the recruits **of Amasa** followed Joab to pursue Sheba ben Bichri. He had gone through all the tribes of Israel **without success in seeking support** until he came to the city of Abel-beth-maachah with all the Bichrites, **his kinsmen. They entered the city and took control of it.** Then they, **Joab and his armies,** came and laid siege against him in Abel-beth-maacah. They built a mount **in the moat** to scale **the walls** of the city. All of Joab's forces began to batter the wall to bring it down.

A wise woman cried out of the city **from the top of its ramparts,** "Hear ye, hear ye, please tell Joab to come here so that I may speak to him." He came close to her and the woman asked:
- "Are you Joab?"
- "I am."
- "Hear the words of your servant."
- "I am listening."
- "In olden days they used to say, 'Take counsel with the people of Abel-**beth-Maacah** and matters will come to a **happy** con-

clusion.' **Even now** we are among the most peaceful and loyal among the Israelites. Would you want to destroy a **substantial** city, **so to speak,** a mother in Israel **as so many villages round about depend on her for their sustenance?** Why would you swallow up a portion of the LORD's people?"

– "The furtherst thing in my thoughts is for me to swallow up or destroy **innocent people.** This is not what I want, only a man from the hill country of Ephraim who has lifted up his hand against the king, against David, Sheba ben Bichri is his name. Only deliver him and I will depart from the city."

– "See then, his head shall be thrown over the wall to you."

The woman went to the townsfolk and argued persuasively so that they cut off Sheba Bichri's head and threw it **over the walls** to Joab. On seeing it, he blew the horn and his men dispersed from the city, every man to his home. But Joab **and the regular army** returned to Jerusalem to the king. **David had heard what Joab had done to Amasa and how without battle he had Bichri slain. He was very angry with Joab, but he said to his ministers, "What can I do with Joab, he is too strong for me to control. Yet, he is loyal. He gave me the city of Ammon Rabbah when he could have conquered it. He defeated Absalom and could have taken the kingdom from me when I mourned for Absalom. I will welcome him as the commander of my armies, for he is this even against my will. But his outrageous slaying of Abner and Amasa cannot be forgiven and the curse I made on him will be fulfilled."**

Joab was summoned to the king's palace. king David stood up to greet him, "You have done well, Joab, son of Zeruiah. You have rid us of Sheba ben Bichri. You will be my commander until I die." So Joab was over all the armies of Israel. Benaiah ben Jehoiada was appointed captain over the Cherethites and the Pelethites, the king's bodyguards; Adoram was over the forced levy; Jehoshaphat ben Ahilud was the recorder; Sheva was the scribe; Zadok and Abiathar were the priests, and Ira the Jairite was David's Prime Minister.[1]

The death of David

Now David was old, at the end of his days. Even when they covered him with layers of clothing he could not get warm. His ministers advised him. "Let there be found for our master the king a young virgin and let her attend to the king and be his nurse. She will lie next to you and our lord the king will be warm." They looked for a beautiful young woman throughout the whole land of Israel. They found Abishag the Shunammite and brought her to the king. The young woman was exceedingly beautiful. She became the king's nurse and waited upon him, but he did not have intercourse with her.

Adonijah ben Haggith, **who was the next in line of succession,** exalted himself for he thought, "I will **soon** be king." He had made for himself horse and chariot and fifty men ran before him, **just as Absalom his brother had done.** His father had never reprimanded him nor said to him, "Why have you acted in this way?" He too, **like Absalom,** was very handsome. He was born after Absalom. He spoke with Joab and with Abiather the priest who agreed to support Adonijah. But Zadok the priest and Benaiah ben Jehoiada, and Nathan the prophet and Shimei and Rei and David's bodyguard, did not support Adonijah **for the king had not yet died.** Adonijah made a sacrificial feast of sheep, oxen

---

[1] This concludes Chapter 20 of the Second Book of Samuel. It is generally agreed that chapters 21 to 24, the final four chapters of Samuel II, are postscripts to the story of David's reign. They include two episodes, both of which raise troubling questions about the workings of a 'benevolent' God, two psalms, ascribed to David (one purporting to be his dying words) and a list of David's mighty warriors. I have put these in the appendix and continue the story line of David's reign until his death from the beginning of the Book of I Kings Chapters 1, 2:1–25.

and fatlings at the Rock of Zoheleth which is by En-rogel to which he invited all his brothers, the king's sons and all the elders of Judah who were ministers to the king, but he did not invite Nathan the prophet nor Benaiah nor the warriors **of David** nor Solomon his brother.

Nathan said to Bathsheba, "Have I not heard that Adonijah ben Haggith has made himself king and David, our lord, has no inkling of it? Now, go and act on the advice I give you, so that you can save your life and the life of your son Solomon, **for if he succeeds and becomes king he will kill you both for he has not invited Solomon to the feast to which he has invited his brothers.** Go to King David and ask him, 'Did you not, my lord the king, swear to your servant, "Solomon, your son will reign after me and he will sit on my throne ," so why has Adonijah become king? While you are still there speaking with the king, I will come in after you and confirm your words." So Bathsheba went into the king's chamber. The king now was very old **and feeble** and Abishag was waiting upon him. Bathsheba bowed down to do homage to the king. He said, "What is your problem?" She replied to him, "My lord, you swore by the LORD, your God, to your servant, 'Solomon your son will reign after me, it is he who will sit on my throne,' and now Adonijah has made himself king, and you, my lord the king, did not know. He has made a sacrificial feast of an exceedingly large number of oxen, fatlings and sheep and he has invited all the king's sons and Abiathar the priest and Joab, commander of the army, but Solomon, your servant, he has not invited. To you, my lord the king, do all of Israel look, to tell them who will sit on the throne of my lord the king after him. If my lord the king lies down with his ancestors **without telling the people who is to be king,** it is I and my son Solomon who will be considered sinners, **traitors worthy of death."**

While she was still speaking to the king, Nathan the prophet entered the court. They told the king, "Nathan the prophet is here." **Bathsheba took her leave of the king.** He entered before him and prostrated himself with his face to the ground. Nathan said, "My lord the king, did you say 'Adonijah will be king after me and he will sit on my throne?' Because he has gone down today and made a sacrificial feast of an exceeding amount of oxen, fatlings and sheep and he has invited all the king's sons, the captains of the army and Abiathar the priest and now they are eating and drinking before him and are declaring, 'Long live king Adonijah!' But I your servant and Zadok the priest and Benaiah and Solomon your servant, he did not invite. Could this matter have been agreed by my lord the king without your informing your servants as to who should sit on the throne after him?" King David answered, "Summon Bathsheba to me." She entered and stood before him. The king swore, saying, "By the life of the LORD who has redeemed my life from all my troubles, I swore to you, by the LORD, the God of Israel that Solomon your son would be king after me and that he would sit on my throne in my place and this will be done this very day." Bathsheba bowed with her face to the ground and she paid homage to the king. She said, "Let my lord, King David live forever." King David gave an order, "Summon to me Zadok the priest and Nathan the prophet and Benaiah." They presented themselves to the king. He commanded them, "Take with you your lord's bodyguard and have Solomon my son ride on my mule and lead him down to Gihon and there let Zadok the priest and Nathan the prophet anoint him king over Israel. Then blow the horn and declare, 'Long live king Solomon.' You will go up after him. He will come in and sit on my throne and will reign in my stead. I ordain him to be ruler over Israel and Judah."

Benaiah answered the king, "So be it. So may it be the will of the LORD, the God of my lord the king. As the LORD was with my lord the king, so may he be with Solomon. May he make his kingdom greater than the kingdom of my lord, King David."

Zadok the priest and Nathan the prophet and Benaiah and **the bodyguards of David**, the Cherethithes and the Pelethites went down and put Solomon on king David's mule and led him to Gihon. Zadok the priest took a horn of oil from the sanctuary and anointed Solomon and blew the horn and all the people shouted, "Long live king Solomon." All the people followed him and they played on flutes and rejoiced with such great rejoicings that the earth almost split by the intensity of their merry-making.

Adonijah and all his invited guests heard **the shouting**. They had finished eating when Joab heard the blast of the horns. He asked, "Why is the city in such an uproar?" While he was speaking Jonathan ben Abiathar, the priest, arrived. Adonijah said, "Approach, because you are a valiant man who always brings good news." Jonathan replied to Adonijah, "Alas, **not so**, our lord, King David has made Solomon king. The king sent with him Zadok the priest and Nathan the prophet and Benaiah, the Cherethites and the Pelethites, and they had him ride on the king's mule. Zadok the priest and Nathan the prophet anointed him king in Gihon, and they came from there shouting with joy and the city is uproarious **with merry-making.** That is the noise you heard. And Solomon now sits on the royal throne. Also, all the king's ministers have come to bless our lord, King David, saying, 'May your God make the fame of Solomon's even greater than yours, and may he exalt his throne even higher than yours.' And the king bowed on his bed. And even so did the king speak: "Praised be the LORD, the God of Israel who has placed my heir on the throne and my eyes have seen it."

All of Adonijah's guests were frightened. They stood up and each man went on his own way. Adonijah was frightened of Solomon. He stood up and went **into the sanctuary** and held on to the horns **which were on the corner** of the altar. Solomon was told, "See Adonijah fears king Solomon; he is grasping the horns on the altar and crying out, 'Let King Solomon swear this day whether he intends to slay his servant by the sword.'" Solomon said, "If he be loyal, not a hair of his head will fall to the ground, but if he is rebellious, he will be found out and die." King Solomon sent this message. They brought him down from the altar. He came **to the king** and bowed to King Solomon. He said to him, "Go to your home. **You will come to my court when I summon you.**"

The day of David's death drew near and he gave these instructions to Solomon: "I am going the way of all the earth. Be strong and be a man! Keep the charges of the LORD your God to walk in his ways, to observe his laws and commandments, his rules and instructions as is written in the Teachings of Moses so that you may succeed in all that you do and wherever you turn, so that the LORD may confirm his promise concerning me: if your descendants walk on a straight path being loyal to me with all their hearts and souls then not one of them shall fail to be on the throne of Israel."

"You also know how Joab acted in defiance of me by what he did to two captains of the armies of Israel – how he killed Abner and Amasa, pouring out the blood of war in times of peace, bloodying the belt around his waist and the shoes of his feet **with innocent blood.** Act wisely but let him not go peaceably in old age to the grave. Be gracious to the descendants of Barzillai the Gileadite; let them be among those who eat at your table because they were very helpful to me when I fled from Absalom, your brother. There is also Shimei the Benjamite from Bahurim for you to repay. He cursed me with unending curses when I fled to Mahanaim, but **afterwards** he came down to the Jordan to greet me **on my return journey to Jerusalem,** and I swore by the LORD that I would not have him slain by the sword. Do not let him go unpunished. You are astute and will know how to deal with him, only send his grey head in blood to his grave."

David then slept with his ancestors and was buried in the City of

David. Now the years that David ruled over Israel numbered forty. He ruled in Hebron for seven years and in Jerusalem for thirty-three years. Solomon sat on the throne of David his father. His kingdom was firmly established.

Hannah's psalm of praise to the Lord

Chapter 2:1–10

My heart exults in the Lord.
My head is held high because of the Lord.
My mouth is made eloquent over my enemies
Because I rejoice in your deliverance.
There is none as unique as the Lord
Because there is no one but you.
There is no rock like our God.

Do not be excessive in boasting.
Do not let your words be arrogant.
Because the Lord is a God who knows **all**.
By him are **one's** actions weighed up.

The bows of the heroes are broken.
Those in full armour stumble.
The bloated hire out their labour for a piece of bread.
But those that were hungry are satisfied.
The barren woman has given birth to seven children,
While she who had many children has become wretched.

It is the Lord who kills and brings life
He brings one down to the grave and raises **people** up.
The Lord determines who will be poor and who will be rich.
He casts down, but he also lifts up.
He lifts up the poor from the dust.
He lifts up the needy from the rubbish tip
And sits them down with princes
To inherit a throne of glory.

The pillars of the earth belong to the Lord.
He has placed the world upon them.

He will guard the steps of his righteous ones.
But the wicked shall be placed in silent darkness
For not by power is man victorious.
Those who rebel against the LORD shall be shattered.
Against them he will make the heavens thunder.
The LORD will judge to the ends of the earth.
He will give power to his king
And lift up the head of his anointed one.

Vengeance against Saul's descendants

CHAPTER 21:1–14

During the reign of David there was a famine lasting for three years. After the first year, David consulted the LORD. The LORD responded: "It is because of Saul and his blood-drenched family who put to death the Gibeonites **after Joshua swore in my name that you would live in peace with them.**" The king summoned the Gibeonites (the Gibeonites were not of the Israelites, but a surviving remnant of the Amorites with whom the Israelites had made a treaty of peace under oath – which Saul had ignored in his ambition for conquest on behalf of Israel and Judah). David said to the Gibeonites: "What can I do for you and how can I make atonement **for what Saul did to you,** so that you can bless and be reconciled to the LORD's people?"

The Gibeonite elders replied, "Our issue with Saul and his family is not over silver and gold nor do we have any desire that any Israelite be killed on our account." He asked them, "Whatever you ask I will do your wish." They said to the king, "The man who was destroying us and conspiring against us so that we would have no presence within the borders of Israel – **it is against him and his house that we require vengeance** – Give us seven of his male descendants and we will hang them **on gallows as penance** to the LORD in Gibeah, **the capital** of Saul, the **so-called** chosen of the LORD. **All of Israel will then recognize the wrong we have suffered at the hand of Saul and his house.**" David replied, "I will deliver **them to you.**"

The king had mercy on Mephibosheth the son of Jonathan because of the LORD's oath between them – between David and Jonathan. But the king seized the two sons of Rizpah daughter of Aiah whom she bore for Saul; Armoni and Mephibosheth and the five sons of Merab the daughter of Saul whom she bore for Adriel ben Barzillai, the Meholathite. He delivered them to the Gibeonites who hanged them on a mountain to the LORD. All seven fell dead **from the gallows at the same time.** They were killed during the harvest season – in the first days of the barley harvest.

Rizpah, **the mother of Armoni and Mephibosheth,** took sackcloth and spread it out for herself **as a tent to cover her** on the rock **where they were hanged** from the beginning of the harvest until the rains descended upon them, **six months later. She kept vigil**[1]. She did not allow the birds of the heavens to touch them during the daytime, nor the field animals at night. David was told about the behaviour of Rizpah the daughter of Aiah, Saul's concubine. **He praised her piety to his ministers;** David then went and took the bones of Saul and Jonathan from the burghers of Jabesh-gilead, who had stolen them from the plains of Beth-shan where the Philistines had hanged them when the Philistines slew Saul in Gilboa. From there he brought up **not only** the bones of Saul and Jonathan but also the bones of Saul's descendants who were hanged **at Gibeah-saul.** They buried the bones of Saul and Jonathan his son in the territory of Benjamin at Zela in the sepulchre of Kish his father **along with the bones of his seven descendants.** They acted according to all the king's commands. After this the LORD was pacified and the land was free of famine.

Translator's comment: This gruesome tale of revenge is a reflection of a period in which individualism was not a concept. A child was the continuation of his father's line – his immortality. By punishing the live child one punished the dead father. The brutality in this tale of vengeance is projected on to God. Because Saul is supposed to have broken the vow

---

[1] The lack of burial was a further punishment. Israelites, like the Greeks, believed that the souls could not rest until their bodies were covered.

made by Joshua to the Gibeonites. God causes a famine. The Gibeonites are therefore only fulfilling God's will by asking for vengeance.

A political interpretation would be that a famine would have been considered to be the fault of the king for not maintaining God's favour – the sole source of natural blessings and curses; that David's court sought to move the blame to the former king, Saul. His war against the Gibeonites becomes the rationalization for the famine. One should note that they do not approach David for redress; he summons them. By this political stroke, David would have achieved two objectives, diverting the people's anger over the famine away from himself, and ridding himself of any potential rival to the throne from the house of Saul. Only Jonathan's son is spared. This is attributed to the pact between David and Jonathan. Remember also that Jonathan's son is crippled and is virtually a prisoner in David's court. This explanation diminishes David's moral stature, but should not for this reason be ruled out as a possibility.

APPENDIX III

CHAPTER 21:15-22

The Philistines went to battle against Israel. David and his officers went down to engage the Philistines. David grew faint **in battle.** Ishibenob, one of the giants of the Rephaim, the weight of whose spear was three hundred shekels of brass – his armour and armaments all being newly made – was about to kill David, but Abishai came to his rescue and struck down the Philistine and killed him. Then David's men swore unto him, "No longer will you go out to war, so that you do not put out the fire of Israel, for were you to die in battle, **our armies would disperse and our enemies would no longer fear us.**

After this there was another battle with the Philistines at Gob; **in that battle,** Sibbecai the Hushathite struck down Saph, also of the Rephaim. In another battle at Gob with the Philistines, Elhanan ben Jaare-oregim the Bethlehemite struck down Goliath the Gittite,[1] the staff of whose javelin was the size of a weaver's beam. There was another battle at Gath in which their champion fighter had six fingers on both hands and six toes on both feet. He was also the son of a giant. When he taunted the Israelites, Jonathan ben Shimea, David's brother, killed him. These four champions were born to the giant of the Rephaim in Gath – all of them fell before David and his officers.

---

[1] The reappearance of Goliath to be killed not by David but by Elhanan causes problems. Was David given the credit for killing the 'mythical' giant, or was this another giant? In Chronicles I, 20:5 we are told that Elhanan slew not Goliath but Lahmi, his brother. An ancient Aramaic translation and commentary says that Elhanan was another name for David.

David's psalm of thanksgiving to the Lord

CHAPTER 22

David spoke to the LORD the words of this poem on the day that
the LORD delivered him from the hand of all his enemies and the
hand of Saul:

The LORD is my rock and my fortress.
>He is my deliverer.
In the God who is my rock
>I take refuge.
My shield, the horn that declares my victory,
>My citadel and my haven of rest,
My helper, you save me from violence.

I cry out: Praised is the LORD
>And I am saved from my enemies.
The waves of death engulfed me.
>The flood waters of destruction overwhelmed me.

In my agony I cried out to the LORD.
>To God did I cry out.
Out of his sanctuary he heard my voice.
>My cries for help penetrated his hearing.

The earth shook and quaked,
>The foundations of heaven moved.
They shook because he was angry.
>Smoke steamed out of his nostrils
And fire from his mouth devoured **the enemy.**
>Burning embers erupted from him.

He brought the heavens down low.
>Dense darkness was beneath his feet.

He rode upon a cherub; high did he fly.
> He swooped down upon the wings of the wind.

The darkness about him, he made into shelters.
> These were the storm clouds of the sky.
From his presence flashes of lightning burst forth.
> The LORD thundered from heaven.
The Most High let his voice be heard.
> He despatched lightning arrows
To scatter the enemy.
> The lightning sent them into a panic.

The channels of the sea could be seen.
> The foundations of the world were revealed
By the rebuke of the LORD
> And the blast of the fumes of his nostrils.

He stretched out his arm from on high to deliver me;
> He drew me out of deep water.
He saved me from my mightiest enemies,
> From those who hated me because
They were stronger than me.

They stood up against me in the days of my anxiety
> But the LORD was my security.

He brought me into spacious places.
> He delivered me because he took delight in me.
The LORD has rewarded me because of my righteousness.
> Because of the innocence of my hands, he has reciprocated.

I have kept the ways of the LORD
> And have not through wickedness strayed from my God.
All his rules were ever before me
> And I did not stray from his laws.[1]

---

[1] This boast is not consistent with David's behaviour.

I was faithful to him
    And held myself back from sinning.
Therefore the Lᴏʀᴅ has repaid me for my righteousness
    Because I was innocent before him.
Towards those who show mercy, you are full of mercy.
    You act justly to men of great integrity.
Towards the pure of heart, you are pure.
    You are malicious towards those who are crooked.

You give assistance to an afflicted people
You keep out an eye for the proud to humble them.

You are my light, O Lᴏʀᴅ.
    The Lᴏʀᴅ lightens up my darkness.
By your powers, I defeat a troop **of soldiers.**
    By **the strength of** my God I scale walls.

As for God, his way is perfect
    The word of the Lᴏʀᴅ is sure
He is a shield to all
    Who put their trust in him.

Who is God, if not the Lᴏʀᴅ?
    Who is a rock, if not our God?

God is my fortress of strength
    Who leads me in straight paths
Who makes my feet swift as those of the hinds
    Who raises me up to the high places.
Who trains my hands for battle.
    So that my arms can bend a bow made of brass.
You have given me a shield of victory.
    Your coming down to me has made me great.
You have made me to walk with giant steps
    And my feet never slip.
I have pursued enemies and destroyed them;

Nor did I return until they were utterly consumed.
I have swallowed them up;
    Defeated them so thoroughly
They will not rise up again.
    They are fallen under my feet.
You have given me the strength to do battle
    You have cowed those who rose up against me.
You made my enemies turn their backs to me **in flight** –
    Those that hate me – that I might cut them down.
They looked **for help** but there was no help!
    Even unto the LORD but he did not answer them.
I pounded them like dust into the ground.
    I did stamp upon them as mud on the streets.
I trod them down
    You have delivered me from the dissensions of my people.
You have kept me as the monarch of nations.
    Peoples who do not know me do serve me.
The sons of foreign peoples dwindle in my presence.
    As soon as they hear about my power, they obey me.
The sons of foreign people melt away.
    And come trembling out of their secret places.

The LORD lives; praised be my rock!
    Exalted be the God – the rock of my victory,
The God who executes vengeance on my behalf
    And makes peoples suppliant to my rule.
Who makes me go out from my enemies.
    You raise me above those who rise up against me.
You deliver me from men of violence.
    Therefore, will I thank you LORD among the nations
And sing praises to your name;
    A tower of deliverance to his king,
Who acts kindly to his anointed one:
    To David and his descendants for ever more.

David's farewell psalm

CHAPTER 23:1–7

These are David's final words –
    The sayings of David son of Jesse,
The sayings of a man elevated to high station:
    The anointed one of the God of Jacob
The sweet singer of Israel.

The spirit of the LORD spoke through me.
    His word was upon my tongue.
The God of Israel said, the Rock of Israel spoke to me:
    The righteous shall be ruler over men.
Only he that rules with respect for God;
    He is as the morning light when the sun rises,
A morning with no clouds.
    As the clearness after rainfall,
When the young grass darts out of the earth.

For is not my house, **my kingdom,** confirmed by God?
    He has made an eternal covenant with me –
Clearly ordered, signed and sealed
    For all my causes and all my wants.
Will he not make them to prosper?

But the wicked they will be as thorns cast away.
    They cannot be grasped by the hand,
And the man who takes them on
    Must be armed with an iron head on a wooden javelin.
They, **the wicked,** shall be burned wherever they be
    Like the thorns and bramble that get in the way.

APPENDIX VI

The heroes of David's kingdom

These are the names of David's mighty men: Yosheb-basshebeth, a Tachemonite, an officer over captains; also, Adino the Eznite **who lifted up his spear** against eight hundred men whom he slew in one battle. Following him was Eleazar ben Dodo, an Ahohite, one of the three mightiest men with David when they put their lives in jeopardy against the Philistines who were mustered there for battle, when the men of Israel had retreated. He stood firm and kept striking down Philistines until his hand grew weary but his hand stuck to his sword. The LORD performed a great victory on that day; and the soldiers returned to him only to strip **the slain.**

Following him was Shammah ben Agay the Ararite. Now the Philistines had mustered themselves into a band in a plot of a field growing lentils, and the people had fled from the Philistines, but he stood in the midst of the field and defended it and smote the Philistines. The LORD performed **through him** a great victory. Three of the thirty captains went down and came to David to the cave of Adullam during the harvest; a troop of Philistines had camped in the valley of Rephaim. David was then in the stronghold and the garrison of the Philistines was then in Bethlehem. David longed **for some water**. He said, "Oh, that one would give me water to drink from the well at Bethlehem which is by the gate **of the town**." These three mighty men, **on hearing David say this, set off and** broke through the Philistine camp, drew water from the well of Bethlehem by the gate and carried it back to David, but he did not want to drink of it, but poured it out as a libation to the LORD. For he said, "This be far from me, LORD, to do this, **to drink this water.** It would be like drinking the blood of the men who jeopardized their lives to fetch this water."

Therefore he would not drink it. Such were the acts of valour of these three heroes.

Abishai, the brother of Joab, was the head of the three men. He raised his javelin against three hundred men and slew them, so did he become famous as one of the threesome. Of the three he had the most respect. Therefore, he became their captain. But he was not as heroic as the **first** three heroes **mentioned**. Benaiah ben Jehoiada the son of a valiant man of Kabzeel who had performed mighty deeds – he struck down two lion-hearted men from Moab. He also descended into a pit during a snowfall and slew a lion. He struck down an Egyptian of great stature who had a javelin in his hand. He went down to him with only a staff, but plucked the javelin out of the Egyptian's hand and killed him with his own javelin. Such were the acts of valour of Benaiah, so did he become famous as one of the threesome. He was more respected than the thirty captains, but was not as heroic as the first three heroes mentioned. David appointed him over his bodyguard.

Asahel, the brother of Joab, was one of the thirty, as was Elhanan ben Dodo of Bethlehem; Shammah the Harodite, Elika the Harodite, Helez the Paltite, Ira ben Ikkesh the Tekoite, Abiezer the Anathothite, Mebunnai the Hushathite, Zalmon the Ahohite, Maharai the Netophathite, Heleb ben Baanah the Netophathite, Ittai ben Ribai of Gibeah of the Benjaminites, Benaiah the Pirathonite, Hiddai of Nahale-gaash, Abi-albon the Arbathite, Azmaveth the Barhumite, Eliah-ba the Shaalbonite of the descendants of Jashen-Jonathan, Shammah the Hararite, Ahiam ben Sharar the Ararite, Eliphelet ben Ahasbai, the descendant of the Maacathite, Eliam ben Ahithophel the Gilonite, Hezrai the Carmelite, Paarai the Arbite, Igal ben Nathan of Zobah, Bani the Gadite, Zelek, the Ammonite, Naharai the Beerothite, armour bearer to Joab ben Zeruaiah, Ira the Ithrite, Gareb the Ithrite, Uriah the Hittite – thirty-seven in all.

APPENDIX VII

The plague over David's census

CHAPTER 24

The LORD was again angry with Israel so he incited David to endanger his people with this thought: "Go number **the men** of Israel and Judah." The king said to Joab, the commander of his army, "Go now among all the tribes of Israel from Dan to Beersheba and count the men so that I may know how many men there are **who can bear arms**." Joab protested to the king, "Let the LORD your God increase however many there are a hundred fold and may the king live to see it happen, but why does my lord the king want this to be done?" But the king was adamant against not only Joab's opposition but that of all the officers of his army. So Joab and his officers departed from the king to count the people of Israel. They crossed the Jordan and camped in Aroer on the right side of the city, that is in the middle of the valley of Gad near Jazer. They then passed on to Gilead and to the territory of Tahtim-hodhsi; then they came to Dan-jaan and round about on to Zidon and then approached towards the stronghold of Tyre, to all the cities of the Hivites and of the Canaanites and they went out to the south of Judah as far as Beersheba. Thus, when they had gone back and forth throughout the country, they returned to Jerusalem at the end of nine months and twenty days. Joab gave the sum total of the reckoning of men **capable of bearing arms** to the king: there were in Israel eight hundred thousand brave men that drew the sword; the men of Judah were five hundred thousand men.

David's conscience made him regret that he had done a census of the people. David said unto the LORD: "I have sinned greatly in what I did. Now, LORD, please pass over the guilt of your servant for I have acted very foolishly. **I counted the men of Israel**

and Judah who could go to battle for me for my own **vainglory.**
Did I not know that my victories were due to you Lord, my God
who delivered me from all my enemies? With your help, I being
few in numbers defeated the Philistines and all the enemies of
your people. I sent my officers against their will to spend nine
months and twenty days to number the warriors of Israel when
only you, O Lord, are powerful to save. Forgive me and do not
let the people of Israel, your servants, suffer on my account."
David rose in the morning **after his prayer.** The word of the LORD
came to Gad, David's seer **in regard to David's prayer:** "Go and
speak to David saying, thus says the LORD. 'I give you a choice
of three punishments, choose one of them and I will do it to
you.'" So Gad came to David and told him, "**What do you choose?**
Shall seven years of famine overcome you in your land or will
you flee for three months before your enemies who will be pursuing you or shall there be three days of pestilence in your land?
Now, consider and tell me how I should respond to him who sent
me." David said to Gad, "I am in dire straits. Let us leave it to
the LORD for great is his compassion, but let me not fall into the
power of men."

So the LORD sent a pestilence upon Israel from the morning even
to the appointed time – **three days** and there died of the people
from Dan to Beersheba seventy thousand men **capable of bearing**
arms. And when the Messenger **of God** stretched out his hand
against Jerusalem to destroy it, the LORD regretted the evil **with**
which he had afflicted Israel and he said to the Messenger that
was destroying his people, "It is enough! Hold back your hand!"
The Messenger of the LORD was then by the threshing floor of
Araunah the Jebusite. David spoke to the LORD when he saw the
Messenger who was striking down his people, "Look, I have
sinned, and I am guilty, but these my sheep, what wrong have
they done? Let your hand strike out against me and my father's
house!" **But God did not answer him.**

On that day Gad came to David and said to him, "Go up and build an altar unto the LORD on the threshing floor of Araunah the Jebusite." And David went up as instructed by Gad as the LORD had commanded. Araunah looked out and saw the king and his ministers coming towards him and he bowed down before the king with his face to the ground. Araunah asked, "Why is my lord the king come to his servant?" David replied, "To buy your threshing floor and to build an altar to the LORD that the plague my people are suffering may end." Araunah said to David, "Let my lord the king take **whatever he wants** and offer what seems good to him. Here are oxen for the burnt offering and the threshing instruments and the wooden yokes of the oxen for fire wood." All this did Araunah wish to give to the king. Araunah furthermore said, "May the LORD your God accept your petition." But the king replied to Araunah, "No, I will buy it from you for a price. I will not offer up burnt offerings to the LORD my God which cost me nothing." So David bought the threshing floor[1] and the oxen for fifty shekels of silver. David built there an altar and offered burnt and peace offerings. So the LORD was pacified on behalf of the land **of Israel** and the plague came to an end in Israel.

POSTSCRIPT:
This is a very moving story. God in a very human-like fashion seems already to be angry with the people of Israel and needs an excuse to punish them. Is David's desire to know the strength of his potential army a reflection of the people's growing smugness at their security since David's victories over their enemies? Does the author want to indicate once again that the Lord, the God of Israel, and not David or

[1] The threshing floor of Araunah the Jebusite according to Rabbinic tradition is Mount Moriah, the place where Abraham took Isaac, his son, to be sacrificed and the site of the Temple. According to Chronicles I, 21:25 the price paid was six hundred gold shekels. This was perhaps intended for the entire area, not only the threshing floor.

his armies, is the source of Israel's security? Is this additional tale a prophetic insert to bring home its message that Israel's salvation depends on God and no one else? Whatever the answer to this question, David's rebuke of God is very moving and still relevant: Why do the innocent suffer for the sins of their leaders?